To Cathy,

May your knowledge and experiences translate into satisfaction and joy !

Craig Parkinson

The Pendulum of Politics

Today's Politics from Yesterday's History

Craig Parkinson

authorHOUSE®

AuthorHouse™
1663 Liberty Drive
Bloomington, IN 47403
www.authorhouse.com
Phone: 1-800-839-8640

First published by AuthorHouse   02/22/2011

ISBN: 978-1-4567-1919-7 (sc)
ISBN: 978-1-4567-1921-0 (hc)
ISBN: 978-1-4567-1920-3 (e-b)

Library of Congress Control Number: 2010919246

Printed in the United States of America
Bloomington, Indiana

This book is printed on acid-free paper.

This book is dedicated to
Mike, Andrea, David, and Sarah,
And especially to Mary!
I love you all.

"May reading stimulate your mind, warm your heart, and soothe your soul!"
  Craig Parkinson

Very special thanks to Verna Thompson for editing.

Table of Contents

Prologue:
The Pendulum is swinging!

Is confederation alive and well in 2010? One would be surprised but the term confederation encompasses more than just the American Revolutionary Era or the Civil War Era. It includes the belief in states rights and limited federal involvement in day to day existence from Independence through today and even into the future. So the answer is yes, the election of 2010 proved as much. **We, as a nation, have developed two distinct philosophies of government. I call them, Confederation and Federalism.**

Federalism includes more of a nationalistic feeling of control through multiple layers of our existence. It is more of an American system of laws that affect all of us. It speaks to more monolithic control rather than regional, state or individual control-it is national. **Federalism does include state and local considerations, but is taken in the context of nationalism.**

Confederation relies on state control. It has joined with other states for the purpose of protection. Confederations may have more concerns in common than just protection; economic and cultural pursuits often provide important ties. The United States under the Articles of Confederation and Perpetual Union united to become independent from Great Britain. The Confederate States of American united to maintain slavery. **Confederation expects that most of the governing will be done by the states; therefore the national government should stay as small and as non-obtrusive as possible.**

Even though a number of Americans have negative feelings when they hear or see the word Federalism, it is not nearly as controversional as Confederation. They exemplify the far ends of our political spectrum and that is why I chose both of them. The Confederate States of America is an example of a confederation and as such will be discussed at some length. This isn't totally about them however; this is more about **a** confederation rather than about **The** Confederacy.

There are always two sides to the story.

From Confederation to Federalism our country has changed directions based on popular demand. We have had in practice at least two major ideas that have been the driving force for our country. People have tended to gather around these two ideas and debated, argued and sometimes fought each other. As like-minded people agreeing on the direction they think is best, they could be called a political party. **They might not even know or consider themselves as a party, but given the agreement of their ideals, they are united as a political party.**

Actually, the first political parties were decided by your choice of whether you wanted to break away from Great Britain or not. People wanting to stay as a part of England were called Tories or Loyalists to the King. People wanting independence were called Patriots, by other Patriots, or a Rebel, by people who were British or a Loyalist. **Well over 1/3 of people living in America at the time of the Revolution did not take a position either way. They were too busy just trying to make ends meet.**

During the Articles of Confederation and Perpetual Union times, politicians were more for their state than for a political party. **If you were from Virginia, in effect, your party was the Virginia Party, and that State got one vote in Congress.**

Parties really developed with the writing of the Constitution. Those for the adoption of the Constitution were called Federalists; those opposed were called Anti-Federalist. This became more apparent in Washington's Cabinet between Hamilton and Jefferson. Although Washington publicly wouldn't take sides, he did side mostly with Hamilton. He had to. **The pendulum as you will see had swung away from the Articles of Confederation and Perpetual Union and towards the new federalist document called the United States Constitution.**

George Washington and most of the founding fathers thought that they didn't believe in political parties. That is why the practice of the second place vote-getter becoming the Vice President is so unbelievably silly to us. In fact, even as late as 1800, when Jefferson and Burr were running as President and Vice President, there was still a fundamental problem with voting by the Electoral College. When Burr got the same number of votes as Jefferson, the votes did not delineate which position each would receive. Burr, instead of acting vice presidential, saw his chance and went for the gold! It was obvious that voters wanted Jefferson to be President but the ballots didn't say that. **Burr, it turns out, was a power-hungry traitor who later tried to start his own country.**

The system was just plain goofy. Alexander Hamilton from New York finally had to persuade some of his colleagues in the House of Representatives to vote for his arch-rival Thomas Jefferson over fellow New Yorker Aaron Burr. This would cost Hamilton. Hamilton convinced a few of his fellow Federalists to turn in blank ballots instead of voting for Burr so that Jefferson would win. Hamilton thought Jefferson would make a better president even though his political views were completely opposite from Hamilton. Four years later, Burr killed Hamilton in a duel. As we look at it today, we can tell that the Founding Fathers really didn't have much experience. They got so much exactly right, how could they mess this up so badly? **Fortunately they did plan for changes and they fixed it with the 12ᵗʰ Amendment.**

Washington, as the figurehead of our Country, could, should, and would, officially stay above the fray between parties.

Thus begins our story of trials and tribulations that seems to dominate every single news broadcast. America, and our destiny, is seen as ideals on a pendulum. They are swinging back and forth, but they are always being pushed by the unreliable political winds.

Sources of Information

Think about the news we hear or see. We have world, national, region, statewide, local, and personal news. The sources also vary from the traditional big networks, magazines, and newspapers, to cable news, talk radio, and even coffee shop conversations. Some of these are expanding their influence but some, such as the big networks, are losing their monopoly on being our source of information. Rapid information in the form of blogs, twitter, Skype, texting, foursquare, and other **new forms of communication makes the trading of information more rapid but without the filters.** Governments and other groups used to spend millions of dollars on propaganda by repeating the big lie syndrome. Think of the Nazis and their campaign against the Jews, or the Soviet Union and its control over the masses in Asia and

Eastern Europe. They could not keep control unless the government controlled information and news dissemination. Think of China, Iran, and especially North Korea today. **Is their access of news the same as ours?**

It doesn't have to be a big government today that uses propaganda. Read some of the blogs etc and look for some radical ideas that are being repeated and repeated. Many of these are in the form of political views. Back in the Cold War, we were wary of disinformation. That is information that sounds like it's true but isn't. We called it propaganda then and we must still be wary of it today. We must be careful to not fall into the trap of having our own views propagandized by anyone, even our friends. **We must make sure our political views are based on facts.**

This really isn't new. Lots of our early political ideas were openly discussed at public gathering places like Raleigh Tavern in Williamsburg, the capital of Colonial Virginia, or in the Green Dragon in Boston. Some of these ideas were spread by the Committees of Correspondence. Major issues were expounded upon in essays like the ones by Tom Paine called *Common Sense* or the *Federalists Papers* by "Publius" better know as Alexander Hamilton, James Madison and John Jay. **For the most part, those essays were examples of Democracy at its best.**

Senator Joe McCarthy in the 1950's insinuating that some one was a communist and then people believing him was probably Democracy at a low point. Being a Communist, in the United States is not illegal now; it is probably not going to be much of a benefit to you, but it is not illegal. In the 1950's, however; just being accused of having some association with a questionable group that possibly had some communist views could cost you your job and even your career. **If you were a recent immigrant you might be sent out of the country.**

In 2010, being accused of being part of a group is usually less egregious. However; one of my students told me that Obama was a Muslim. I replied, "If he is, that is his business. It is not illegal to be a Muslim in the United States. Obama has said he is a Christian and he got critized for attending a Christian Church for a long time where the Minister was considered to be a radical preacher. You can't criticize him for being both". That is an example of someone, probably a parent, sharing propaganda. **There are lots of legitimate reasons that the parent could have used to express their political beliefs, but we** want our voters to make investigated, educated, and hopefully intelligent choices.

That is why we have free public education. The Congress under the Articles of Confederation and Perpetual Union did a great job of creating the Land Ordinance of 1785. Land was divided into townships; each township would have 36 sections, each a square mile and one of the sections in each township would be reserved **to support public education.**[1]

Before the Civil War only Vermont and Massachusetts had mandatory or compulsory school attendance laws. Horace Mann, a famous educator from Massachusetts said, "If we do not prepare students to be good citizens…if we do not enrich their minds with knowledge, then our Republic must go down to destruction."

American students are deemed to be behind students from other countries in Math and Science. With more emphasis being placed on those subjects, I hope that we don't neglect the Social Studies. To have a true Democracy that works, we must have an educated public. **As the maxim of history states, "those who don't study the mistakes of the past are doomed to repeat the mistakes of the past."**

Confederation or Federalism a Continuing American Struggle

While teaching an 8th grade American History class in 2009-2010, I could not believe how clearly these two philosophies repeatedly stood out in our History. Granted, I had not taught American History for a few years, but as I went through the school year, so many ideas jumped off the pages at me. Always the most obvious were the ideas that make up our two party system. The sides may change, but the views are remarkably the same. In this writing, I will try to justify or explain these changes but for now the evidence shows that the United States has from its inception been involved in a gigantic, epic, and continual struggle of wills for control. **Be it local or national control, it is still a struggle going back and forth in the American conscience like a very large pendulum of politics.**

In doing the research for this book, I found many sources that were prejudicial in their wording. I have tried to police that in my findings and my own writing, but we all have our beliefs. I believe that we should be more concerned about what is accurate than what is tainted as prejudicial. Too many of the bloggers of today have to resort to basic name calling in the discussion of politics. Notice the underlying immaturity of such writings. **They even add some little caricature device to enhance their opinions or some message-loaded nick name as a handle.**

I realize that caricatures and exaggerations in political campaigns are not new. In the election of 1840, many new innovations were used. William Henry Harrison, a son of a Virginia planter made it look like he was a man of the people by giving out whiskey bottles in the shape of a log cabin. He claimed to be the victor in a stalemated battle with the Indians at Tippecanoe, yet he actually left the Army before the War of 1812 was over. Times had been tough and the blame had fallen on his opponent, President Martin Van Buren. Van Buren didn't deserve credit for the Panic of 1837 but he did little to end it. His followers came up with a lasting slogan that did not have much effect on the election of 1840 but has been used in everyday speech since. Martin Van Buren was a native of Kinderhook, New York. In order to counter slogans like "Tippecanoe and Tyler too," or "Van, Van, is a used up man!" Van Buren's staff came up with "Old Kinderhook, he is **O.K.**" **We commemorate the political campaign of 1840 every time we use that phrase. Now you know where the much used saying "O.K." actually came from!**

There was a code of conduct at Iroquois tribal meetings. Some of the rules of proper meeting etiquette were to speak one at a time, and to listen to the speaker with no shouting or interrupting. **"The purpose of the speaking was to persuade not to argue."**[2]This system was developed from the unification of the Iroquois by Hiawatha around 1570. We have many things we can still learn from others. **I subscribe to the Iroquois position of persuasion based on facts and not repeating and repeating loudly, the big lie.**

Finally, I tried to end each paragraph with a significant thought and to put emphasis on that thought, I have emboldened it. **Today's politics is based upon yesterday's history.**

Chapter 1   American Independence

The American situation is unique in the world. The creation of colonies so far away from the existing government gave rise to a more independent administration of those colonies. The slowness of communication from London to the New World was a major factor. The fact that many of these colonies were started as business ventures and not just a new area to govern was also a factor. Several of the colonies were started by religious refugees, or at least we can call them dissidents from the majority of mainstream religious population; that too was a factor. For 150 years, the colonies made a bundle of money for the investors and the crown. That changed because of the world wide conflict with France in the 1760's. We call it the French and Indian War. In Europe, it is know as the Seven Years War. Even though Great Britain won, their financial coffers became strained and the government looked for tax relief from all of its subjects not just the home folks. **It was the failure to ask us, the colonies, for the right to tax us, that was one of the major issues leading to the dissolution of our political ties with Great Britain and the beginning of our Independence.**

Ben Franklin's cartoon showing most of the colonies as a cut up snake. Notice that the colonies kind of follow the shape of the actual coastlines. This was drawn in 1754 to unite the colonies against the French and Indians. It has been adapted and reused many times. The idea comes from a colonial superstition that a snake could come back to life if reunited by sunset. No information was found on why Georgia and Delaware are omitted from the map.

It all began with taxes

By being English subjects, the colonists felt that they had to abide by English Law but also they were entitled to enjoy the Rights of Englishmen. One of the most important laws had been in effect since 1215 when the English nobles forced King John, (the infamous Prince John of Robin Hood legend) to sign the Magna Carta. The Magna Carta said among other things, but most importantly, that the "King could not raise taxes without first consulting the Great Council of nobles and church leaders."[3] **Later, this Council was called Parliament.**

Early on in the colonies, there was an under current against taxes as the Anglican Church was a state sponsored church and as such, got funds through taxes. People of other faiths or non church going people were still liable. In colonies like Massachusetts, being part of the church was required in order to be able to vote. In this light, it is even more remarkable that around 1750, Jonathan Mayhew, a minister in Boston, is reported to have been the first to say "no taxation without representation." In 1765, James Otis of Boston is sometimes given the credit when he said; "Taxation without representation is tyranny!" Most of the members of the British Parliament and the Kings Council thought that the colonies did have representation just like women and children who could not vote had representation, something called "virtual representation"[4]. **It is obvious now that the colonists didn't agree.**

Thus taxes played a pivotal role in our story. Nobody likes taxes but everybody wants the government to do something during a crisis. Modern politicians routinely bring up the cry of no new taxes but they seem to omit the part, "without representation." Many people of today think the colonists were against all taxes and thus they should be. In fact, this belief is shown in some of the ads for debt relief and settlement of tax claims that appear on some current T.V. channels. They all seem to demand immediate action if some disaster happens to hit their state. I wonder if they focus on where that money actually comes from. Proof that the colonists would pay their taxes comes from a line of the Liberty Song. It was written in 1768 by John Dickinson the future author of the Articles of Confederation and Perpetual Union.

"Chorus: In Freedom we're born and in Freedom we'll live.
Our purses are ready. Steady, friends, steady;
Not as slaves, but as Freemen our money we'll give."
Dickinson's lines state that they will pay but only as free men.

John Dickinson believed that we would only succeed if we placed the good of the nation above our own concerns.

One of the first taxes on the colonies was the Sugar Act of 1764. This was a tax on molasses that was imported from the Dutch or French West Indies to make rum in the New England distilleries. The distillers thought the tax would cut too deeply into their profit margin. The other tax was the Stamp Act of 1765. They were taxes to help pay 1/3 of the cost of having around 10,000 soldiers to protect the colonies from attacks by the French, Spanish and the Indians after the French and Indian War. They were also required to outfit the troops with bedding, cooking utensils etc. This was passed in England "in 1765 with less opposition than a turnpike bill."[5]At this time, a turnpike is synonymous with a road or highway today; later on a turnpike became a toll road. So the inference was that the Parliament didn't think that these taxes were any major issue. Boy, were they wrong. Opposition to this tax in the colonies led to the Stamp Act Congress. The Congress brought representatives from nine colonies to New York where they met and wrote petitions to the King and to Parliament. The petitions were largely ignored but the boycott of English goods that cut trade by 14% was not ignored by the British. The Stamp Act was repealed, but new taxes passed called the Townsend Acts. Regardless of the tax, the point was still the same. **No taxation without representation was the colonial claim and Great Britain maintained the right to tax the people in its colonies.**

All of this cajoling was bringing the colonies closer together. It forced them to organize. They joined groups like the Sons of Liberty or the Daughters of Liberty. Later Sam Adams organized the Committees of Correspondence. Boston was the seat of most of the turmoil so Great Britain sent troops there to help keep things under control. The presence of the troops just riled up the citizens of Boston more. One evening on March 5th 1770 a young lad made some disparaging remarks about a British soldier and the soldier retaliated with the butt of his gun. Angry townspeople started to gather and there were more words and some snowballs hurled at the troops.

Paul Revere's engraving of the Boston Massacre was actually absconded from fellow patriot Henry Pelham. Revere got his copies made and to the street faster. It was sent around to all of the colonies with the intent to incite them. Notice the fallacies of this engraving changing the truth. Captain Preston of the guard looks like he is ordering the troops to fire. The troops respond with an organized volley. The building behind the troops is not Butchers Hall. It is taking place in daylight and not at 9 p.m. The dead patriot closest to the troops is Crispus Attucks, an Afro-American made to look white. Even the colonial dog didn't run away from the fight even with gun fire.

Hugh Montgomery: Was one of the convicted British soldiers, (a private) who after his conviction and punishment admitted that after he was knocked down he yelled "Damn you, Fire!" 5 Bostonians were killed in the ensuing fire from the British Soldiers before Captain Preston could stop them. This incident is known as the Boston Massacre. Future President John Adams was Hugh Montgomery's lawyer. **This showed that colonial concerns were not with the British People but with the King and the British Government.**

The Boston Tea Party was a statement against a tax on tea that had been passed in Parliament for which the colonists did not have a single representative. It was passed in part to help the huge East India Tea Company that was nearly broke. Great Britain lowered the cost of the tea because so much was being smuggled into the colonies from the Dutch at a much lower price. The East India Company had warehouses full of tea and they also had powerful lobbyists to get Parliament to make a new deal. The new price was lower than the Dutch even when including a small tax on the tea. The price didn't matter as not only did the colonists throw the tea overboard, they also boycotted the buying of tea from the British. Dressed as Mohawk Indians, the Bostonians didn't damage any other cargo on the ships; they just unloaded the tea directly into the bay. **Nine days later, another "Tea Party" happened in Delaware.**[6]

Drinking tea or the classical 'tea time' has long been a British tradition. The boiling of and drinking of tea in the colonies was practical in some places because of poor water purity, so a boycott was a major individual commitment. The colonists took the taxing without representation very seriously. The British didn't have a clue and after the tea parties, Great Britain felt that they had to enforce the law. The situation just kept escalating. What would have happened if Great Britain would have granted the colonist limited representation in Parliament? Let's say if the British would have granted the colonies one member of Parliament or better yet, one member per colony? Would one member per colony really have upset British political power? **I think that solution would have worked better for Great Britain and would have been cheaper than losing the American colonies in a very expensive war.**

Chapter 2   The ascendancy of Confederation and its downfall

Because of our experience with a strong, despotic and authoritative centralized British government, the new and independent former colonies, fought for and institutionalized a confederation of states. These states basically thought themselves to be independent, but collected together to fight against British tyranny. They had been brought together by the Committees of Correspondence and the Sons of Liberty. And when shots were fired at Lexington and Concord, a new country was born; it was governed by the Second Continental Congress. Even though it began as a loose association of states, still the Congress assumed command of the army and placed George Washington as Commander and Chief of the Continental Army. This was done even before the Declaration of Independence was written. The colonists were gradually becoming Americans. **Very early on the colonists realized that the only hope they had of survival was dependence, (not independence) upon each other.**

Great Britain helped us by fighting a regional war trying to defeat the American rebels. They greatly underestimated our resolve and the British were unable to coordinate an all out attack on America. Basically, the British first attacked the American Colonies in New England, then in the Middle Colonies and finally in the South. They never could get it together. They could win battles but Washington and the army would get away. When all seemed lost, a surprising victory like at Trenton would keep the Revolution going. Although no one area completely carried the burden, it was easier for the Continental Congress to raise money in one area if the British were attacking there. Finally, with the help of the French, Washington and the Continental Army defeated Lord Cornwallis at the battle of Yorktown and for all practical purposes ended the Revolutionary War. **After being victorious in the revolution, however; we were left with a mountainous debt.**

In John Trumbull's painting of the surrender of the British one can see George Washington to the right. Lord Cornwallis was too indisposed to surrender. His second in command, General O'Hara tried to surrender to the French Commander Comte de Rochambeau to the left. He would not take the surrender. Next O'Hara tried to give the surrender sword to Washington, he also refused. Finally because he was also second in command, General Lincoln received the surrender ending for all practical purposes the war. As the British laid down their arms, their band played the song, 'The World Turned Upside Down!'

The Continental Congress had begun to think of ways of governing as the Revolutionary War began. They asked the states to write new constitutions. This was done in most states by simply adjusting the state charters by eliminating all reference to the crown and in some states adding a Bill of Rights for the citizens. With these models in hand, John Dickinson[7] from Pennsylvania penned a majority of the rules of the new government. It is known as the Articles of Confederation but its official name is the Articles of Confederation **and Perpetual Union**. Each state had one equal vote and before anything could be done, 9 of the 13 states had to agree. The Congress was in charge and it was a unicameral, that is, it had only one house in the legislature. Today, only the State of Nebraska operates its legislature with the unicameral form. It took a while for it to be signed as Maryland held out until all of the states that had claims of westward expansion gave up those claims. **Maryland officially signed the Articles on March 1, 1781.**

Constitutions are common place now but The Articles of Confederation and Perpetual Union were remarkable for a couple of reasons. The Articles were the first written constitution of a major area, a country. They had a novel idea of separating the supreme power of a state. **The articles called for a division of power between the states and the nation.**

The government under the Second Continental Congress and eventually the Articles of Confederation and Perpetual Union operated successfully during a war, without money, without a model to use as a guide and through the actions of people who had little experience in national self government. Compared to other revolutionary governments in History, the Articles of Confederation and Perpetual Union was very successful. **The contemporary French 'Reign of Terror' revolution would be the best example showing, by comparison, the success of the Articles.**

However: many short comings of the Articles were soon very apparent. Every state was equal regardless of the number of people or the value of its territory. It had no Executive or Judiciary rule and it could not tax nor regulate commerce. For example, if two states quarreled about borders or trade, who would solve the problem? Who was in charge? Most of the time, it was Congress who was in charge. To get action from any group can take time and get complicated. Like the old saying says, "A camel was a horse created by a committee." **The more views on a committee, the longer and more complicated the issue becomes.**

Robert Morris, as Congress's treasury chief, tried to get the government the ability to tax in the 1780's. [8]The rules of changing the Articles required all 13 states to agree. Morris could get only 12 as Rhode Island refused. Rhode Island, alone, also refused a creation of a National Bank. [9]The paper money that had been issued by the Continental Congress became less and less valuable until the common derogatory saying was, **"not worth a continental."** John Jay as the leader of the Continental Congress in 1779 said "Taxes were the price of liberty, the peace and safety of yourselves and your posterity." Later, feeling a bit deflated he said, **"America had no sooner became independent than she became insolvent."**[10]

Washington and his army dealt with monetary problems during the entire war. This finally reached a head as several officers held a meeting on March 15, 1783 in Newburg, New York. This is known as the Newburg Conspiracy.[11] The army was stationed in Newburg watching the British who had not left New York City yet and waiting for the finalizing of the Peace Treaty of Paris, to officially end the war. The soldiers had not been paid in a while and many were spending their own money to survive. The meeting was just getting started when General Washington entered and surprised the men and asked if he could speak a few words. His speech did not make much of a difference but a few words before the speech began did. Washington as he got his glasses out, he asked the men if he could use his spectacles "for I have not only grown gray, but almost blind in the service of my country." **Most of the officers had never seen Washington with glasses and the realization that he, Washington had sacrificed as much if not more than any of them, left hardly a dry eye in the room and ended the controversy.**

Besides settling the western land's border problems and the organization of the Northwest Territories, not much memorable progress was made by the United States under the Articles of Confederation and Perpetual Union. The new United States was not given much respect by other countries. We had trouble getting the British to leave their forts after the Treaty of Paris was signed in 1783. Spain negotiated a treaty restricting our use of the Mississippi for a number of years (20-25) but the Congress fortunately failed to ratify it. Great Britain refused to negotiate a trade agreement in 1785. Most Americans nowadays probably don't even realize that we had the Articles…**More importantly, many of the people who were working with the Articles, knew that they didn't work very well and that they had to be changed!**

Chapter 3   The Rise of Federalism

A new and stronger national government was needed. Under the new Constitution, a strong statement for Federalism was made. Federalism can be defined as a division of power between the states and the national government with more emphasis on the national government. The states under the Articles of Confederation and Perpetual Union were stronger than the national government. The states, by signing the United States Constitution, gave up some of their powers to the United States government and kept some of their powers. Power in the new government was further divided into three branches of government. They are the Legislative, Judicial and Executive branches with checks and balances to keep each branch from becoming too powerful. **This was the basis for the new government and each branch in turn would have its impact on increasing the power of both the federal government and the policies favoring more states' rights, limited government and in general basic confederation beliefs.**

A national judicial branch was created to check the powers of the President and to interpret what the laws passed by Congress actually said. The Supreme Court has been used by both sides in our discussion. Early on, the Supreme Court didn't realize the power that it had. It wasn't until 1803 that the Supreme Court, led by John Marshall (a Federalist), declared that the court had the power of judicial review. That is, after the ruling in *Marbury v. Madison* 1803, the court had the right to judge whether or not a law passed by Congress was constitutional. The law, the court ruled on, was the very first one passed by the Senate creating the make up of the Supreme Court. The ruling only dealt with part of the law. **Since then the Supreme Court has been a very powerful tool for both sides of our discussion.**

The Marshall Court went on to strengthen the Federal government with many rulings, some of which are mentioned in the following. The very first case was settled out of court just by the pressure of realizing the court agreed to hear it. It was *VanStaphorst v. Maryland* 1791. In 1793, the ruling in *Chisholm v. Georgia* was that the State of Georgia could be sued; the result of that case was the 11th Amendment, changing the U.S. Constitution. This lesson evidently was missed in Iowa in 2009 after the Iowa Supreme Court ruled that the laws of Iowa allowed for same sex marriages. Certain right wing conservatives wanted to go after the court and change the members for their vote on the issue. They missed the idea: the court **interprets** what the law says. **If any group wants to change the ruling, all they have to do is to change the law.** (In the Republican landslide of 2010, the justices were replaced and partisan politics has now been introduced as evidence in the court).

In 1810, the *Fletcher v. Peck* ruling said that the Supreme Court could rule on constitutionality of State Law as it pertains to the United States Constitution. The *Martin v. Hunter Lessee* case of 1816 established the Supreme Court as superior over state courts in dealing with federal matters. The 1819 case of *McCulloch v. Maryland* established the power of the 'Necessary and proper clause' of the constitution where states could not tax the national bank even though the national bank was not mentioned in the Constitution. *Gibbons v. Ogden* in 1824 established the interstate commerce clause. Finally in *Schenck v. U.S.* 1919, Chief Justice Oliver Wendell Holmes Jr. ruled on free speech when he said that even though we have free speech, that doesn't mean we can "yell fire in a crowded theatre" because it invokes the **clear and present danger**. Holmes went on to say that you can't say even a true statement if it would cause a dangerous situation. Successive courts ruled less in favor of the federal government in such cases as Dred Scott, and *Plessey v. Ferguson* which will be discussed later in the book.

There have been times of struggle between the three branches of government. Most notably Congress and the President, he has his veto power and congress can hold up appointments and the passage of legislation that the President favors. Congress can also impeach the president. Two famous cases of that are Andrew Jackson and Bill Clinton. Both were impeached by the House of Representatives but neither was forced to resign by the Senate. **Richard Nixon most likely would have been impeached and removed but he resigned before the impeachment process could work.**

The Supreme Court has had three major run-ins with Presidents. FDR wanted the number of justices changed from 9 to 15. The Court had ruled some of the New Deal laws to be unconstitutional. During the Civil War, Abraham Lincoln was suspending the 'writ of habeas corpus' to hold dissidents without saying why. Supreme Court Justice Taney ordered Lincoln to stop. Lincoln ignored that order which could have been an impeachable offence. With a war going on and the army actively fighting, no one was going to impeach the president. **This practice has continued by future presidents who claim National Security as the reason to break the law.**

What do John Marshall and the Liberty Bell have in Common?
When Marshall died in 1835 they rang the Liberty Bell and that is when it reportedly cracked! The bell has cracked several times and was even recast. The wide crack was an attempt to keep the crack from expanding from vibrations. Weather the story about Marshall and the bell is true or not, both

have been important stories in American History. The bible quote on the bell is from Leviticus 25:10 saying "Proclaim liberty throughout the land unto the inhabitants thereof." In their own way, both Marshall and the bell have done their job and their legacy lives on.

Probably the most famous case was the argument between Chief Justice John Marshall and President Andrew Jackson. Marshall was against the mandatory removal of the Indians of Georgia. Jackson was for it. After Marshall had ruled against it, Jackson is reported to have said, "Now that Marshall has ruled against it, now let him try to enforce it." Clearly it was an impeachable offense by President Jackson. The voters in the state of Georgia were for it and so was the vast majority of Congress. **Nothing was done to Jackson.**

An executive branch with some checks and balances was also created in the U.S. Constitution. George Washington of course was elected President. He created a group of people to help him. They each headed up a department. They were the departments of State, Treasury and War along with the offices of Attorney General and Postmaster General. One of his cabinet posts was the Department of the Treasury. It was headed by Alexander Hamilton who promoted the federalist idea of giving value to our money system and to create a national currency.[12] This meant taking responsibility for all of the state's debts. This was not popular with some of the Southern States who had already repaid most of their debts. **As a compromise, Washington, the nation's new federal capital city, was to be built in the two southern states of Maryland and Virginia in an area now called the District of Columbia.[13]**

Even with this compromise, more and more federalist ideas were becoming so predominant that the people in the government supporting them were called Federalists. Some of the people, who disagreed with them, were Thomas Jefferson and James Madison, who were joined by New Yorkers Governor Clinton and Aaron Burr. At first these people who disagreed with adoption of the new Constitution were called the Anti-Federalists.[14] Soon after the adoption of the constitution, they started to call themselves **Democratic Republicans and then just Republicans which can be confusing today as the Democratic Party can actually trace its lineage back to this group but not the modern Republican Party.[15]**

Since Hamilton believed in a national bank and that the Federal Government must pay off all state debts, what was the financial balance sheet? The national debt was $77,228,000 and expenses to run the government were $4,269,000 in 1789-1791.The amount of income from tariffs was $ 4,399,000 plus $19,000 for a total income of $4,418,000.[16] That amount seems to be an insurmountable amount. Think of how that compares with the size of our debt today! **The debt was gradually reduced and financial stability established by a popular tariff on foreign goods and by an unpopular tariff on Whiskey.**

Why Whiskey? Was that really that big of a product in America? Actually the farmers found that making corn into whiskey allowed it to be transported easier than the bulky unprocessed corn. Remember, the transportation system had not been revolutionized by canals and railroads and turnpikes yet. It was just plain easier to transport barrels. Hamilton insisted on this tax as a way to show that the Federal Government could tax internally. After some fairly violent resistance to the tax, President Washington called on the militia to end the Whiskey rebellion. **Hamilton had gotten exactly what he wanted. A show of force by the Federal Government over the states and the people, and Hamilton was happy.**[17]

Chapter 4   The Pendulum swings back

Not everybody was happy however. Many of Hamilton's ideas were rejected by Washington's Secretary of State, Thomas Jefferson. Jefferson and Hamilton become the key figures in our struggle. **In fact, the different sides of this political question are sometimes referred to as the Jeffersonian or the Hamiltonian side**.

When Thomas Jefferson became the third President of the United States, the Federalists were scared of what could happen to the government. Would the government go back to the malaise suffered under the Articles of Confederation and Perpetual Union? Jefferson did change many Federalist programs but he tried to down play the political party factionalism. Jefferson was a big believer in the theory of Laissez Faire. That is the French phrase meaning that government should basically keep their hands off or stay out of business affairs. Jefferson cut back the government along with asking Congress to repeal the whiskey tax. He also cut back the military. **Jefferson, however, was convinced by his Secretary of Treasury, Andrew Gallatin, to keep the United States Bank, a very Federalist idea.**

The Federalist movement faded in power when Jefferson became president. The Federalists lacked vibrant new leaders and were controlled by Alexander Hamilton. **In 1804, former Vice President of the United States, Aaron Burr, and Alexander Hamilton fought a duel and Hamilton was killed; basically, so was the Federalist Party.**

Thomas Jefferson, who is sometimes credited with starting the Democratic Party believed in a strict interpretation of the Constitution. One of his dilemmas as President was how to justify the purchase of the Louisiana Territory from France in 1803. It was a great purchase and a necessary one. Where in the Constitution does it give the President the right to purchase more land? Jefferson finally decided that a purchase is really a treaty and the Constitution gives the Senate authority to approve that action. **So, Jefferson made the buy and the Senate approved the Treaty outlining the purchase of the Louisiana Territory.**

Chapter 5   Nullification Theory

Jefferson deserves another look for contributing to the rise of the Confederation. Besides his credit for writing the Declaration of Independence, Jefferson brings up the theory of nullification. In 1798 President Adams and the Federalists in Congress passed the Alien and Sedition Acts. This gave power to the president to expel any foreigner and to change the immigration law to keep some one from becoming a citizen for 14 years instead of the existing law of 5 years. The Sedition Act made criticism of the government or its officials illegal. Jefferson and fellow Virginian, James Madison, (who is considered the Father of the Constitution) chose to fight these new laws. **Instead of taking this problem to the U.S. Supreme Court, Jefferson and Madison took this to the states, seeking to have the states nullify the Federal Law within their state's borders.**

This is a radical and important precedent. The right of the states to nullify the national law is an important cornerstone to the Confederacy. Why did Jefferson and Madison do this? Did they consider nullification because they really believed that nullification is the state's right? Or did they do this because the Supreme Court, which had not established the Power of Judicial Review yet, was made up of predominantly Federalists? Regardless, in 1798-99 the States of Kentucky and Virginia passed nullification resolutions. These resolutions also served another purpose. **So many copies were printed, that they were used as campaign brochures for the presidential election of 1800.**

Thomas Jefferson & John Adams.

Thomas Jefferson and John Adams had lots in common. Both were delegates at the 2nd Continental Congress. After Jefferson wrote the Declaration of Independence, Adams read it to the Congress. Jefferson didn't have the greatest speaking voice and Adams was much better. Adams pushed the Congress to accept the wonderful writing of Jefferson. In 1778, they were fellow diplomats in France. When George Washington became President, Adams was the Vice President and Thomas Jefferson was the Secretary of State. That is when a rift was started. Jefferson believed in smaller government and Adams believed in Federalism. Their conflicting views boiled over when Jefferson was Adam's Vice President from 1796 to 1800. Jefferson lost by just a few votes. Early in our history, the person getting the second most votes became the Vice President. Jefferson narrowly defeated Adams in the 1800 election. After both men had retired, Adams began writing to Jefferson and they were able to patch things up and become great friends. The spirit of competition remained as Adams swore to out live the younger Jefferson. Adams died thinking that Jefferson was still alive but in fact, Jefferson had died just hours earlier. **The date was, July 4, 1826.**

Thomas Jefferson was elected President. He served for two terms followed by James Madison's two terms as President. **Was this coincidence or just good politics?**

This is a great example of how things change but are really still the same. In Arizona in 2010 a conservative movement to regulate immigration has been challenged by the Federal Government. So today, we have Federalism challenging Confederation whereas in 1798 we had Confederation challenging Federalism over basically the same issue but the parties have switched sides. **For any political buff this has to be exciting stuff,**

After the War of 1812, the British began to dump many of it goods for sale here in America at bargain prices. This was killing American industry which had really gotten going during the war. Congress began passing a series of protective tariffs to raise the price of these imported goods. The South, who sold most of its cotton and tobacco to Europe, objected to these laws. The cost of buying manufactured goods was more because of the tariffs. It looked as though the laws were designed to help manufacturing in New England at the South's expense. This pattern continued and in 1828 the highest tariff was passed and John C. Calhoun tried to use the nullification theory again. Calhoun was Vice President. Do the states have the right to limit the power of the Federal Government? Calhoun thought so since the states had created the Federal government. President Andrew Jackson, a southerner, disagreed with Calhoun so Calhoun resigned as Vice President. It was not over however. Calhoun soon was elected Senator from South Carolina. In 1832 a lower tariff was passed but South Carolina was still not happy. They passed a Nullification Act and threatened to secede if challenged. President Jackson asked for a compromised tariff proposed by Henry Clay, at the same time getting a Force Bill into Congress allowing him to use force against South Carolina if they should try and secede. **No one came to South Carolina's side and the issue was put away, continuing to fester for 28 more years.**[18]

Maybe the theory of Nullification, worked for the election of Jefferson and Madison and Calhoun and got the tariff reduced, but I don't believe that it was really believed by others to be a legitimate theory. I say this because neither side tried to implement it when it really counted. The North, if this was believed in, could have simply invoked this theory into practice when any Fugitive Slave Law cases would be brought up for trial. The Northern States could have simply nullified any law dealing with returning runaway slaves to their owners. This would have restricted any travel outside the slave states by slave owners bringing their slaves along. It would also not impose slave owning beliefs on states that did not believe in owning slaves. Many Southerners felt that because it was in the Constitution, there was nothing wrong with bringing slaves into territory where the residents had an opposing view about of slavery. **Too often states' rights advocates, like so many people, only see one side, and that side is theirs.**

Since South Carolina threatened nullification in response to the tariff of abominations in 1828, and if nullification was a true and practical theory, why did South Carolina secede from the Union in 1860? No laws had even been presented to change the slave driven economy of South Carolina. The balance of power in the Senate had changed but even then if some future law was passed, South Carolina could simply nullify it and South Carolina would continue along its way as the states' rights advocates insist is their right. President Jackson had threatened military action against secession but nothing had ever really been done against nullification. Why did South Carolina want other states to come along and form another country? What part of states' rights deals with the advocating of forming another country? **If you think that you are independent, then act independently.**

This dissatisfaction with national government policy has not been just in the South. It has also occurred in New England and by former strong Federalists. The War of 1812 had caused undue hardship on New England and a group met in December of 1814 at Hartford, Connecticut, to consider, of all things, secession from the United States. The debate centered on the closure of New England's harbors due to the British blockade. If the war was successful, the new lands would make other sections of the U.S. more powerful than New England and thus New England would lose its influence. **While debate continued, the war ended; that ended the blockade and hence ended the debate in Hartford**.

As our country grew, we experienced growing pains called Sectionalism. Nullification would be one ailment of Sectionalism. Protective tariffs for one area, at the expense of another, were almost fatal as we shall see. Sectionalism plays an important role in the nature of politics. Sectionalism is large enough to possibly survive as a country but not diverse enough economically to prosper with a changing of circumstances. Thus New England was susceptible to a naval blockade to eliminate trade. The South was also susceptible for the same reason just with different products. The West (Midwest today) was tied to the Mississippi and controlled by the Port of New Orleans. The Far West was isolated by the vastness and roughness of the terrain. That is why developments like the Pony Express, telegraph, the Union Pacific

Railroad, the discovery of gold and the Panama Canal were vital ties keeping all of our sections together in the United States. **The chant USA which unites the nation, although unstated, can also mean the United Sections of America.**

Before the inclusion of the Far West and those developments, an effort was made at conciliation of sections. President Madison had the idea and Henry Clay championed it. It was called the American System. It was a plan to have protective tariffs and to use that money to develop infrastructure such as roads and canals. Reconstituting the National Bank would help trade with a nationally accepted currency. A National Road, financed by the national government was tinkered with. Many other improvements were made. The Erie Canal worked so well that New York City became America's busiest port with products from the Great Lakes converging with products off of ships from all over the world. **With all sections of the country included, is it any wonder why this time is known as the Era of Good Feelings.**

Chapter 6   Jackson

Sometimes, the strength or weakness of the person who is President decides the direction in which the pendulum swings. Andrew Jackson was such a man. Stubborn might be one of his attributes. As a child of 13, he and his brother were captured by the British during the American Revolution. When he refused to shine a British officer's boots, he was hit and his faced slashed. While he has quite a colorful past, most of that doesn't deal with our topic. He was bold and tough as his nickname of 'Old Hickory' implies. He was elected from the new state of Tennessee, first as a Congressman and then as a Senator. He resigned to become a Supreme Court justice of Tennessee. He worked and built up his plantation home called the 'Hermitage.' Starting with just 9 slaves he ended up with over 150. Being the commander of the Tennessee Militia, he was called upon during the War of 1812. He battled against Indians inspired by Tecumseh. In 1814 he defeated the Indians at the Battle of Horseshoe Bend. Davey Crockett and Sam Houston served under Jackson there. He concluded a treaty that gave 20 million acres of Indian land to the U.S. to be settled by Whites. He was then called upon to defend the port city of New Orleans from the British. Facing his biggest challenge, a victory would make him forever famous.

Using a rag tag combination of troops including Free Blacks, and Baratarian Pirates under Jean Lafitte, Jackson took on troops that had just defeated Napoleon. The British lost 2,057 killed including 3 Generals, compared to 13 Americans. [19]Technically, it was not the most decisive victory in the War of 1812 or any war. **The peace treaty ending the war had been signed in Ghent, Belgium but the news had not yet reached New Orleans. The war was already over.**

Jackson would be a political power from now on. In 1817 President Monroe sent Jackson to Georgia to deal with some Indian trouble. The Seminole Indians attacked Jackson, so he attacked their villages and crops. Spain and Great Britain were agitating the Seminoles. Without orders, Jackson attacked in Florida, a province of Spain. **When Spain protested, Jackson said that Spain should either garrison Florida to keep control or cede Florida to the United States. They ceded Florida.**

In 1824 the Democratic –Republicans were by far the strongest party but they ended up running four candidates for President. They were Speaker of the House, Henry Clay, Secretary of State John Quincy Adams, Treasury Secretary William Crawford and Jackson. Jackson got the most popular vote and Electoral votes but not enough to be named

President. The election went to the House of Representatives where John Quincy Adams was named President; Adams subsequently named Henry Clay as Secretary of State. To many people, this didn't look right. This became known as the 'corrupt bargain.' Jackson won the next two elections easily and he invited everyone to the White House. He was the first President of the common people. Jackson also was the first President that really expanded the powers of the presidency. He <u>led</u> his party to accomplish legislation instead of asking for approval from Congress. **Someone once called him a "Jackass" and he liked that and even used it for a while. Later, cartoonist Thomas Nast used it again to represent the Democrats and it stuck.**

As tough as "Old Hickory" was, his second administration was upset by something called the "Petticoat Affair." Secretary of War Eaton, with Jackson's approval married the recently widowed Peggy Timberlake. Vice President Calhoun's wife and Jackson's niece who served as what we now call the First Lady and other women snubbed Peggy because she had not waited long enough to remarry. In the end, just about everybody resigned from the cabinet leaving Martin Van Buren to be the next in line to become president. It would be a gift of questionable value, although in 1835, the economy had gathered such a surplus, the national debt was paid off. **Jackson became the only President to be President when there was no national debt![20]**

Jackson was a man of many seeming contradictions. Jackson, who supported slavery but defended fiercely the Union, caused the removal of thousands of Indians across the Mississippi but had an adopted Indian child. The most noteworthy removal of Indians was the Cherokee's 'Trail of Tears.' In 1835 a crazy man pulled two guns out and tried to fire at close range at Jackson. Both guns misfired. That was the way Jackson had lived his life. Having survived 13 duels, numerous battles, and the saber scar on his face, "Old Hickory," had dramatically increased the power of the Presidency. **It is getting harder and harder to find candidates to live up to his veracity.**

I said that it was a questionable gift of becoming President for Martin Van Buren. As President he faced a serious recession caused by furious fighting over the United States Bank by Jackson and Bank President Biddle. Simply, other banks and states issued paper currency and some of that money had questionable backing of it. Jackson issued an executive order saying all Federal land purchases must be paid for with specie (paper money) that was backed by gold or silver. Land values had been expanding. States, that had been receiving surplus funds from the Federal government and had started major projects like canals and railroads, lost the surplus funds. At the same time Great Britain had a depression so cotton sales lagged and we then had a balance of trade deficit. To top off the Panic of 1837, there were crop failures. This was all based upon the rising prices of the Indian land that had been forcefully taken from them and put on the market. Unemployment skyrocketed and so did the national debt. Various similar things happened during the Great Depression of 1929. Good times were followed by questionable investments, poor weather, and lack of confidence. Jackson had fought so hard against a national bank and then the results turned out to be so bad. It is questionable if the bank could have prevented the Panic. **Some people might blame the taking and selling of Indian land as the cause; maybe it was just greed**.

Chapter 7   Manifest Destiny

Where has the Spirit of Manifest Destiny Gone?

The belief that Americans should, could, and would expand across the country from coast to coast has dominated the American psyche from colonial times on. Thomas Paine in the Pamphlet *Common Sense* talked about "continent" and not just colonies. With the addition of Hawaii and Alaska as states, two related questions must be asked. Did the addition of Alaska and Hawaii signal an end to, or completion of Manifest Destiny? If not, **where is that spirit going to lead us?**

Manifest Destiny got an early start in the colonies. Several colonies claimed land all the way to the West Coast. Great Britain proclaimed in 1763 a "Proclamation Line." It was basically the ridge line of the Appalachians. This was to keep better control of the colonies. It would stop the conflicting claims by the colonies and it would allow for some cooling down time for the Indians. **For all of their stated reasoning, it was a huge land grab by the Crown.**

After the revolution, the Articles of Confederation and Perpetual Union government passed the Land Ordinance of 1785, organizing that territory to become future states. During Jefferson's Presidency we had the fortunate opportunity to purchase the Louisiana Territory in 1803. In 1819 by the Treaty of Adams-Onis we received Florida from Spain and paid $5,000,000 yet gave up any claims on Texas due to discrepancies resulting from the Louisiana Purchase. The Monroe Doctrine written by John Quincy Adams but delivered by President James Monroe in December of 1823 set the tone that it would be the United States watching over the Americas and not Europe. In actuality we were not in much of a position to do anything about it. Great Britain saw an opportunity to open many new Central and South America markets that had been closed to them. **Their navy actually**

restricted Europe as many Latin American countries gained their political independence and the financial independence to trade with anyone. **Before their independence, they were required as a colony of Spain to trade with Spain.**

The question over the Oregon territory that had been held jointly by Great Britain and the U. S. since 1818 was settled on June 15th 1846 with the boundary agreed upon to be the 49th parallel. People had been calling for "54 40 or fight" using the lower boundary of Russian Alaska. The British public didn't care and Robert Peel was headed out of office as the British Prime Minister. He made us an offer. **The United States was at war with Mexico at the time and decided on a quick settlement.**

The United States and Great Britain almost came to blows in what is known as the Pig War. The Oregon agreement didn't exactly mark the border within the San Juan Islands in what is now Washington State. 13 years after the agreement on June 15, 1859 the two groups were living on the island and a British-owned pig ate some potatoes out of an American garden. The Angry American shot the pig. The British wanted compensation for the pig. Arguing over the price, things started to escalate; soon the British had 5 war ships and over 2000 men, and the Americans had 461 troops and some cannons. Captain George Pickett of future Gettysburg fame is reported to have said, "We'll make a Bunker Hill out it." British Rear Admiral Robert Baynes was ordered to land and attack. He refused saying, "two great nations in a war over a squabble about a pig is foolish." A joint military occupation was agreed upon until the boundary could be settled. A third party agreed with the Americans in 1872. **Today the National Park Service continues to raise the Union Jack over the former British camp.**

In the *Democratic Review* of 1845 John L. O'Sullivan wrote complaining of foreign interference and attempts aimed at "limiting our greatness and checking the fulfillment of our manifest destiny to overspread the continent..." That is the first recorded use of the term, 'Manifest Destiny.' I doubt if any country including Great Britain was worried about our greatness, but **it did give a name to the feelings that most Americans had.**

Ohio Representative Duncan said that he had a fear of the centralized federal government. The best way to fight that fear was through expansion. He said, "To oppose the constant tendency to federal consolidation, I know of no better plan than to multiply the states, and the further from the center of federal influence and attraction, the greater is our security." Duncan didn't plan on the development of the telegraph, railroads, or the ingenuity of the Federal government. **Of course he didn't count on our modern technologies but he also didn't foresee the problems of the expansion of slavery and the resultant Civil War, a war that skyrocketed Federalism**.

The feeling was ripe to fulfill our destiny of being a nation from coast to coast and we had the opportunity. The independent Republic of Texas wanted to join the United States. Most people were for it except those who were anti-slavery and those who didn't want to go to war with Mexico. There was a boundary dispute between Texas and Mexico. Mexico said that the southern boundary was the Nueces River. Texans claimed it was the Rio Grande. It was easy to set a trap for Mexico by placing troops south of the Nueces River. Mexican troops attacked our troops and gave us the excuse to declare war on Mexico. President Polk asked Congress' approval and they did. We won easily but it cost us nearly 13,000 lives, mostly from disease, and $97.7 million. We signed the Treaty of Guadalupe Hidalgo giving us territory all the way to the West Coast, settling the Rio Grande as the official border of Texas. **Many Civil War figures got practical hands on experience in the Mexican War including Jefferson Davis, Robert E. Lee, and U.S. Grant.**

As luck would have it, James Marshall, working for John Sutter in California, discovered Gold in January of 1848. **Manifest Destiny was complete and there was a pot of gold, literally at the end of the rainbow**.

Feelings for expansionism are always on the rise after easy little wars such as the Mexican War and the Spanish American War. In the aftermath of costly, major bloody conflicts, the mood is different. **After the Civil War, WWI and WWII there was little feeling of expansion and more for a rise in isolationism**.

After both World Wars, we kind of let our guard down resulting in further conflicts. As we became a Super Power, we needed to flex our muscles. Germany after WWI and USSR and China after WWII took advantage of our isolationism. Even the expansionism after the Mexican War and the Spanish American War brought problems. The Mexican War land secession was a contributing cause of the Civil War. Our territories gained by the Spanish American War have proved difficult. **In the end, Cuba and the Philippines were granted their independence and we learned that it is difficult ruling colonies.**

Chapter 8 Confederacy

A Flawed System

The Confederate States of America fell to the same fate as the Articles of Confederation. They were doomed from the start with a flawed system of government. The biggest flaw is that a country must have a way to force the payment of taxes, dues or membership fees. It also has to have a national defense. A national defense with local control equals an oxymoron and thus a poor system. By having a national tax system of some sort and a national defense program it ceases to be a pure confederacy. **It is to the South's credit and the North's chagrin that the South survived as long as it did.**

For weeks I have struggled with the problem of justifying that a confederacy is a flawed system. The most obvious difference in the U.S. Constitution and the Articles of Confederation and Perpetual Union was the balance of power in the national government, namely the absence of the executive and judicial branches. This theory had a major defect. America, under the Articles of Confederation and Perpetual Union did not have an executive but won the war of Independence. The Confederate States of America did have an executive but lost the Civil War. Both Confederacies faced a stronger opponent and did not have much of a chance at surviving. Both had great military leaders in George Washington and Robert E. Lee. To help me to try and find the answer I looked for another example of a loose association of independent states, I found the perfect example in the United Nations. The United Nations has a weak executive with a very strong Security Council in control. The purpose of the United Nations is to try and prevent wars and try and improve the human conditions on Earth. **All three Confederacies have had financial problems.**

The Soviet Union early on in the history of the United Nations made a very big mistake. In trying to show a protest over the topic of discussion concerning communism in Korea, The Soviet delegation stormed out of the Security Council meeting where they held the power of a veto. While the Soviets were out, the council voted unanimously to send troops to fight in a police action in Korea. Miffed and embarrassed at their diplomatic goof, the Soviets retaliated by not paying their dues to the United Nations. Since this was our opponent in the Cold War, and since the purpose of the United Nations was to prevent a hot war, the United States picked up the tab. **Thus, I found the weakness of confederations is the inability of a confederacy to demand and enforce payment of dues, taxes, membership fees etc.**

The Roman, Cicero said "There is no fortress so strong that money can not take it."[21] Senator Robert Byrd said "Cicero's astute observation is timeless. What force will temper the executive if they control the purse strings?" Byrd was talking about a system of checks and balances where the legislature controls the "purse strings" and not the executive. The inference is clear. Not only is this true for federalism's system of checks and balances, but also a confederacy's inability to get money in a consistent and plentiful manner.

This control over the money has been the key all along. In 1215, the Magna Carta was signed separating government powers requiring the King to ask for taxes. Earlier the English and others paid a "Danegeld." That was tribute to the Vikings who were led by Danish Kings and the payment kept them from attacking England. The Roman had taxes as Jesus said, "Give to Caesar, the things that are Caesar's and give to God, the things that are God's." Darius the Great from Persia in 500 B.C. collected taxes as did the Pharaohs in Egypt 5,000 years ago. **All of these countries could and did collect taxes but the Confederations could not on a national scale.**

Chapter 9   In Defense of the South

Mistakes made early in the development of the South doomed it to the destruction of the Civil War. The South chose an agrarian society; which by itself would have been fine, but I believe that with the addition of slavery, the combination sealed the South's destiny. From the beginning at Jamestown some form of profitable enterprise was needed to justify the colony's existence. Lacking gold, the colony got off to a rocky start. Tobacco was the life saver of the Jamestown colony. As more of the South was occupied, rice and cotton proved profitable. **With the addition of slavery and Eli Whitney's invention of the cotton gin, cotton profits soared. (Cotton gin was short for cotton engine)**

As evidenced even in early times in Virginia's House of Burgesses, most elected officials were planters. Some of our most famous leaders of the new republic were such and especially note worthy were George Washington and Thomas Jefferson. As this trend continued, I believe that the social elite specialized in improving profits of cotton and tobacco and not branching out into other risky ventures such as manufacturing. This caused several limitations to continue.

1. Leadership of the South was tied to promotion of cotton and tobacco. By keeping the status quo, they would become and stay wealthy but dependant.
2. Because the labor force was slaves, non slaves of poor economic backgrounds would not immigrate to the South. The economic opportunities for new faces were limited.
3. The pressing need of development of economic alternatives was absent.
4. With cozy trade relations with cotton hungry Great Britain, the need to develop manufacturing was stunted. In business

it is good if both the buyer and seller can make money. **That relationship makes for long term complacency**.

This then was the economic trap that the South found itself in. The trouble started when the more populous North needed to prop up the new fragile industries with a protective tariff. This happened several times. Sometimes we were at war with Great Britain, the largest and most consistent trader with the South. This caused a double whammy as the manufacturers of Great Britain built up big inventories during wars and embargos. After the resumption of trade, there would be sellers' marketed discounts and American industries would need to be protected again. Besides the protective tariffs, government expenses needed to be paid for. **The Federal Government used only protective tariffs, and excise tariffs to get money. They would also sell federal land. Other means of taxation were not thought possible because it hadn't been conceived or wasn't seen as being appropriate or even constitutional.**

The second law passed by the new Congress was the Tariff act of 1789. It taxed imports at rates between 5-10%. In 1790 it was raised to 7-10%. In 1792 it was raised again but a discount of 10% was given if it was shipped on American ships. The Dallas Act of 1816 was a tariff to help pay for the expenses incurred in the War of 1812. The new tariff rate became 10-15%. **In 1824 Western and Northern interest joined together to raise the tariff again.**

In 1828, southern congressmen came up with a strategy to defeat the next round of tariff hikes. They added more tariffs to more products by amendments. The plan was to make it so large and hard on everyone that it would not pass. When the vote came, the Northeast voted 16-23, the South voted 3-50 but Tennessee and Kentucky voted 12-9 and the West 17-1 and the Mid- Atlantic states voted 57-11 to carry the vote 105-94. **The South got beat at its own game and they raised their own taxes to new heights. They were mad and embarrassed and they weren't going to pay this <u>Abomination</u>! That is why the tariff of 1828 was called the Tariff of Abominations.**

South Carolina was threatening to secede but their leader John C. Calhoun was Vice President and Southerner Andrew Jackson was the new President. Thinking that these southern leaders would be helpful the South just complained. The tariff caused a rift between Calhoun and Jackson and in 1832 when the new tariff was not substantially reduced, Calhoun, now a Senator from South Carolina, threaten to use nullification to stop the tariff and there was more talk of seceding. **President Jackson got Congress to reduce the tariff by 2% per year for 10 years. He also ordered the army to be ready to occupy South Carolina if they tried to secede.**

In 1842 the Black Tariff, as it was called, raised the tariff back to 40% but trade dropped 20% as Great Britain reduced the amount of cotton that it purchased due to world events. The Black tariff was repealed in 1846. All of the tariff negotiations were like a painter painting themselves into a corner. **The South still had plenty of room and they were out of paint but they were about to get a big new bucket of paint called Texas.**

Because of growing crops such as cotton and tobacco that rob from the soil, expansion was needed. Texas would fill the bill nicely except war with Mexico would undoubtably happen and the United States would undoubtedly win and with that would be more land, probably California. The problem was political. The South already was greatly outnumbered in the House of Representatives but even in the Senate. With the new territory, more non slave states would come into the Union and the Senate, and the House also would be lost forever. Southerners felt that bills such as the Wilmot Proviso would be raised and raised again until it passed. It had called for the elimination of slavery in the new territory received from Mexico and had been narrowly defeated. The annexation of Texas did allow for the subdivision of Texas by Texans if they wanted to help stem the tide of more Free states verses Slave states. **Besides that being the last political hope for the South, there is not much evidence of who supported that subdivision, least of all Texans.**

The chess match was about over and the South had only a couple of moves before they were to be checkmated. The four reasons stated earlier now limited the South in preparation for war. Less immigration meant fewer men available for the army. Just raising and selling cotton meant that an embargo by blockade would take away income and possible trade for armaments. Without factories, it would be difficult to get or make war material. **So, without some new and dramatic invention, or an offer to buy all of the slaves, war was the only option left and it wasn't a good option.**

In retrospect, specialization is short sightedness. Specialization sets you up for a disastrous situation if the key elements change. Diversification and research and development have to be continuous. Black Smiths used to be in great need until every one owned a car. A ferry boat operation could be profitable until a bridge was built. Potatoes will grow in poor Irish soil until a blight attacks them. It is not easy to look forward and see the many pit falls ahead. **What dangers lie ahead of us?**

Chapter 10   The Confederate States of America

The Confederate States of America never really had a chance as a nation. The creation of this entity was almost always in a war time existence. It had to be done quickly and in order to survive; it had to go against some of its own principles. It had to be a nation of States' Rights, a belief that each state was basically an independent nation but it also had to carry on a Federal war. Throughout the Civil War, The Confederate States of America struggled with national currency, the writ of habeas corpus, a national draft, and in the beginning had basically one party. **The political party wasn't really organized as such, but for all practical purposes, it could be called the Confederate Party.**

Jeff Davis didn't stand much of a chance as leader of such a party while trying to manage a war. With all his faults that writers have bestowed on him, he still survived and so did the Confederacy for four war years. Without other political parties, Jeff Davis's decisions became the focal points of political bantering, typical of opposing political parties. Soon the euphoria of the secession began to wane and Jefferson Davis found himself dealing with 11 (one from each state that seceded) political parties as states' rights came more and more to the forefront. In the U.S. "to the victor belong the spoils" had been the system for many government appointments. The party out of power didn't expect appointees. After Jefferson Davis made an appointment, 10 other parties questioned the choice. Davis tried to be politically correct in his appointments even though the creation of the Confederate Government happened at a very rapid pace under extraordinary circumstances. With the emergence of the 11 party system, every decision and appointment came under greater and greater scrutiny. Abraham Lincoln's struggle with finding a general that could really lead the North to victory has been greatly chronicled. **His problems, although paramount to the North's success, pale in comparison to Jefferson Davis'.**

Jefferson Davis was keenly aware of his position and tried to spread around all of his political appointments from his cabinet, to the military- all in deference to the 11 different states. With many disappointed parties Davis came under more and more scrutiny. His popularity waned and as the war ground on, Davis had another problem. His name was Robert E. Lee. **Davis came to really respect Lee but Lee's rise of popularity and esteem, while absolutely earned, was partially gained at the expense of the President of the Confederacy.**

Although the Confederate system was and is flawed, the idea of local control is still very powerful, and it has endured to this day. **That is why I believe that the Confederacy is alive and well today.**

This idea is not based on the popularity of such Confederate icons as The Stars and Bars flag or grey hats or the reverence for such figures as Robert E. Lee or Stonewall Jackson. Though the number of sales is still very high even during a major recession and the number of web sites is growing, what intrigued me were the ideas behind the confederate cause. What really happened and what has been perceived to have happened. With the war over, the North went on to other endeavors. To the South, it was over. The only thing left for the survivors, was to write about it. Several southern historical societies sprang up and wrote their side of the story. In his book, *Dixie Betrayed*, David Eicher, explains how the romanticized and glorified cause of the Confederacy has been promulgated. **He ends his book with the conclusion that "together they, (the leaders of the south) formed an imperfect union, and together they (again the leaders of the South) destroyed it."**[22]

In Gary Gallagher's book, *The Confederate War*, [23]he defends the South and tries to show many examples of how the South didn't really give up and how some people never gave up. He is perplexed at why non-slave owners in the south would fight so hard and use so much of the resources to fight for slavery. The answer is simple: each individual had their own reasons for fighting, and as Americans, I would expect nothing less than supreme effort from them. Funny isn't it, there isn't a book on how hard the Union fought. I believe that after the first couple of battles the soldiers on both sides fought fiercely. Granted the Union soldiers didn't have the same concerns at home as the Confederates nor did the civilian population of the North. Too often we get tied up by emotions on our choice of beliefs. How did the Japanese people last so long as we beat them back to Japan and we had to resort to the Atomic Bomb twice to end WWII? Or, what were the beliefs of the American home front in fighting so hard in WWII? **The answer is of course they fought hard, it was WAR!**

I firmly believe that by outfitting and transporting both armies from the Civil War, they could have easily conquered any country, **any army or combination of armies anywhere in the world in 1865.**

Chapter 11   Slavery: A Way of Life in the South

For this writing, I am going to use the premise of slavery as a necessary way of life for the South. This is not necessarily a Confederate view but most Southerners could not imagine a South without slavery. It may be difficult for us in the 21st century to really comprehend a typical Southern slave owner's feelings about the slaves. Most slave owners did not think that their slaves were equal human beings. Some of them didn't even think of them as human beings. I believe that if the Southerners would have thought of slaves as equal human beings, it would have been harder to intellectually justify the institution of slavery. Think about that as you read part of a famous speech by Patrick Henry (a Southerner) in prerevolutionary times. "Is life so dear, or peace so sweet, as to be purchased at the price of chains and slavery? Forbid it, Almighty God! I know not what course others may take; but as for me, give me liberty or give me death!" [24]**If Patrick Henry felt that way about it, why wouldn't all men?**

A way to justify that institution would be to dehumanize the slaves. This would not be too different than our 20th Century depiction of the Germans (Huns) in WWI [25]and the Japanese (Japs) in WWII. Slavery had been around for a long time in the colonies and peoples attitude of seeing one group as educated and successful and another as uneducated, deserving to be restricted and ordered around does not lend itself to feelings of fairness, equality, or even freedom. Sometimes I liken the feelings about slaves to the way farmers feel about their farm equipment today. Some farmers like a certain type of tractor. Some take better care of their tractors than others. Some develop a kind of feeling toward their machinery. **They cuss it when it breaks and praise it when it**

works well. They have a shed to keep it in. Sometimes they trade it and sometimes they buy more.

Slaves were the method and means of farming. I know that that is a rough comparison at best but remember that slavery didn't just start up all of a sudden. One big difference that was always in the back of each owner's mind was keeping control of the slaves. They had to make them work hard in order to make more money. They had to keep them from running away. Slaves were valuable and allowing runaways could lead to more runaways. In many areas, slaves equaled or outnumbered whites. **They had to keep the slaves from being able to form any resistance that could grow into a full-fledged revolt.**

Slavery became an acquired necessity when the financial benefits clouded the issue and almost all of social mores condoned the issue from the beginning of the colonies. Georgia struggled early under James Oglethorpe's decree of small farms and no slavery. Profits soared later with the arrival of large plantations and slaves. [26]The Carolinas were a good area to grow rice. Rice farming needed lots of workers, so in the early 1700's, most people coming to Charleston, were black slaves to do the work. This even caused the separation of the area into North and South Carolinas. **North Carolina was not as conducive for growing rice. However; North Carolina would gain more slaves when tobacco and then cotton became the preferred crops for profit.**

Some people believe that slavery would have phased itself out with the development of new technology. The agricultural shift to growing more corn for example might have had a big effect on the role of slaves. Corn, with more of a hierarchy in levels of production would give some of the slaves an elevated status. With a differential of slave responsibilities, more education, training, and decision making would give slaves more opportunity for advancement. **Tobacco and cotton production lend themselves to menial, non-progressive, repetitive jobs.**

Evidence of invention however shows the complete opposite reality. The value and number of slaves before the invention by Eli Whitney of the Cotton Gin was significantly less and because of the invention it was tremendously increased. It stands to reason that Cyrus McCormick's reaper would not have affected cotton or tobacco as it did grain crops. The mechanized cotton picker was not refined until the mid 1950's. Its development came after years of competitive experimenting and developing. It came at a time of great need as many black farm workers had gone on the "Great Migration." Starting in the 1920's and going into the 1960's, thousands of African-Americans migrated to the manufacturing cities of the north especially Cleveland, Toledo, Detroit and Chicago.[27] They migrated to escape Jim Crow laws and take jobs that were available because of the interruption of European immigration that had traditionally filled the labor voids in these northern areas. This caused a considerable labor shortage in the southern cotton industry. This of course happened in a time when African-Americans could choose where they lived and worked. During slave days choice was not possible and other adjustments by slave owners would have maintained control. Why couldn't slaves be used to run the new inventions? I believe that slave owners would have been very creative continuing to use slaves to increase or at least maintain their profits. **Regardless of your opinion of slave owners, they were business men.**

In 1860, slavery was still very profitable, and needed to expand in order to meet demand and survive. "Cotton was King" as Southerners proudly stated. I think that the planters/ruling class in states that needed slavery to continue their way of life could see the writing on the wall. With California in the Union, the number of Free States outnumbered the Slave States and that trend looked irreversible. Slavery as an institution was in danger. Great Britain had renounced slavery in the 1830's and the opinion of the world was changing. The end of slavery was a just a matter of time. However, all was not lost; Great Britain still bought slave grown cotton and tobacco. But the question still remained, **how long could slavery last?**

A dark and brooding reason for the expansion of slavery into the territories was the birthrate of the slaves. Without expansion, the number of slaves would continue to rise and would increasingly dwarf the white population. A fear that all slave holders had was of an armed slave rebellion. With some of the planter class being educated in the classics, they knew of the Greeks of Sparta and how they were so physically strong and austere just to keep their slaves (helots) under control. They also knew of the Roman's Spartacus and his slave rebellion that defeated Roman armies. Without going to the ancients, the slave owners could just remember Nat Turner. Turner's attempt at rebellion in 1831 cost 57 whites their lives. **Of course, John Brown's raid at Harpers Ferry**

in 1859 and the attempted slave rebellion epitomized the greatest threat to slavery. That threat was from outside agitation.

Just think about how different American History would be without slavery. It almost happened. Thomas Jefferson, in the proposed Land Ordinance of 1784, abolishes slavery in the new territories after 1800. **It failed by one vote!**

Chapter 12 Firestorm

Expansion of Slavery was the powder keg and the election of Abe Lincoln was the match that set off the firestorm.

The election of 1860 sent shock waves throughout the South. They thought that it was now time to act. The election was one of the most remarkable in American History. It was different from the normal premise of two opposing ideals and thus two political parties as in most of our elections. Two major political parties is central to American History. Some of the elections have been by a small margin and some have had a third party, but by far, most elections are decided between two parties. The few exceptions are James Monroe's Era of Good Feelings second term in 1820 and of course both of George Washington's elections. Those elections were on the opposite end of normal as there was little opposition or even differing points of view. **The election of 1860 offered 5 basic points of view for the same question.**

The question was of slavery and its expansion. The Democrats met in South Carolina and the issue of expansion of slavery split them into the Northern and Southern Democrats. Some people formed the Constitutional Union party to try and keep the country together. The Republicans picked Abraham Lincoln, backing the idea of not allowing any new slavery. The Abolitionist's obviously wanted to end slavery. Of the 5 groups only 4 had a presidential candidate. The Abolitionist's did not have one so they voted for the candidate with the closest view to theirs. Thus, with such a division, Abraham Lincoln carried the election. He was not even on the ballot of 10 southern states and yet he was still able to win. **The country had a regional president and he was not from the South.**

Chapter 13 Right of Succession

Reasons and rationale for Southern legitimacy for Secession and arguments against that rationale

Many writers, officials and even historians, both now and then, claim that slavery was not the issue. I would just like to refer them to a comparison of the U.S. Constitution and the Confederate States of America Constitution with readings of the Declaration of Independence and the Articles of Confederation and Perpetual Union.

Most often, the reason for the rationalization for secession is found in the Declaration of Independence. The phrases "whenever any form of government becomes destructive to these ends it is the right of the people to alter or abolish it and institute a new government." Later in the document it says, "But when a long train of abuses and usurpations, pursuing invariably the same object, evinces a design to reduce them under absolute despotism, it is their right, it is their duty, to throw off such government." The reasons for secession would be: 1) the tariffs that helped the Northern manufacturing 2) the election of Abraham Lincoln, (who expounded no new slavery in the new territories) and 3) lack of enforcement of the fugitive slave laws. Based on these assumptions, I find these to be very weak arguments for secession. They help the ruling class of the South which is made up primarily of slave holders. Maybe their reasons are better outlined in their states' documents explaining why.

If one is going to use the Declaration of Independence as reasons legitimizing secession, which really only declared us independent from Great Britain, the last line of the first paragraph says that, "they should declare the causes which impel them to the separation." **South Carolina's rendition is called the "Declaration of the Immediate**

Causes Which Induce and Justify the Secession of South Carolina from the Federal Union."[28]

They actually passed one on April 26, 1852, but deferred to the wishes of the other slave states to wait. Their biggest arguments were that former land, north of the Ohio River, that had been claimed by Virginia had been voluntarily given up to the government under the Articles of Confederation and Perpetual Union and that Virginia would not have given up that land had it known that slavery would be outlawed there. Even if that were true, what concern is that for an independent nation of South Carolina? That would be a concern for Virginia. They also stressed concern for the geographical line drawn across the country marking slave territory and free territory. Again, none of that land was in South Carolina. They reported an anti slavery invasion meaning the infamous raid on Harper's Ferry led by John Brown. Again, Harper's Ferry is in Virginia. (The people responsible for that raid were killed or executed by the U.S. Government). The opinion of most of the Northerners was against slavery and some Northerners thought that John Brown was a hero. **True as that might be, if South Carolina was an independent state, how can they dictate how any other state should think, believe, or feel?**

The lack of compliance for the fugitive slave law was a big concern. Several northern states had laws trying to ignore the enforcement of the Fugitive slave laws. The last time I checked, South Carolina was surrounded by slave states that should have captured run away slaves before they got to the Northern non- slave states. The *Dred Scott v. Sanford*, United States Supreme Court Case of 1857, ruled in favor of the slave states. The states that tried secession did have representation in the United States Congress based on equal representation in the Senate and based on population in the House of Representatives. The southerners even had 3/5 of certain 'property' counted for representation. **At the time of the secession, the President of the United States was a Democrat and most Southerners were also Democrats.**

The stated reason, even before the election of 1860 was to secede if Lincoln was elected. One of the reasons stated in the South Carolina declaration said "with the election of a man... whose opinion and purpose is hostile to slavery." Lincoln's "House divided can not stand" speech really scared the South. This seceding was more of a proactive, preemptive move. Mississippi thought that they would lose 4 billion dollars if they lost the slaves. They were also concerned about slavery in only less than half of the Louisiana Territory. Georgia thought that they lost out on potentially 3 billion dollars worth of property in the new territories. Again, check a map. Mississippi and Georgia, if independent states who were able to secede, they could hardly claim new territory as slave territory without action by the whole federal government. You are either a part of the United States, where you are entitled an equal say in the Senate or you are an independent country of which territory belonging to the United States is of no concern of yours. Texas had three main issues that were a bit different from other slave states. They were concerned with 'Bleeding Kansas', lack of protection from Indians on their western borders and being bordered by seceding slave states. States' Rights champion Tom Jefferson struggled with buying the Louisiana Territory, **where were the States' Rights concern with annexation?**

So what were the long train of abuses and usurpations? What had the North seized without right? The Declaration of Independence listed 28 paragraphs of specific abuses by the King. Do we hear more about abuses, or Lincoln's election and how he was going to free the slaves? And another, we volunteered to join the Union, so we can volunteer to leave the Union! Speaking of volunteering, if you joined almost any army in the history of the world, would they let you back out any time you wanted? **For all the claims for states' rights, their own arguments are for expansion of slavery.**

Going back to an earlier era, we can look at our first constitution that was signed by South Carolina. South Carolina is again chosen here because it was the leader of the secessionist states. The official name of this document is "The Articles of Confederation and Perpetual Union." **Perpetual Union, why is it that the Perpetual Union part hasn't been stressed or taught in our schools?** Even though the United States Constitution has supplanted the Articles of Confederation and Perpetual Union as our official law of the land, it was a building block to our constitution.

South Carolina and the others violated the letter of the Articles by having a meeting to discuss secession because under Article XI they needed consent of the U.S. Congress before such a meeting can be held. Article IX says that "congress is the last appeal to a problem." Article XIII states **"and the Union shall be perpetual."**

Now, in fairness, Article II says that "the States retain sovereignty, freedom, and independence." What is the intent of the Articles? The confederation allowed each state to be sovereign inside its borders, and independent inside its borders, and have freedom inside it own borders. Since the Articles were replaced, what exactly is the position of the official law of the land, the United States Constitution? The preamble starts out by saying "for a more perfect Union. "Under Article 1, Section 10, Powers denied to the States, Part 1, it says, **"Unconditional Prohibitions, no state shall enter into a treaty, alliance, or confederation."** Part 3 says, "No State shall without the consent of congress…enter into any agreement or compact with another state or engage in war **unless actually invaded**." Article 4 states that, "The United States shall guarantee to every state a republican form of government."

That brings us to the 10th Amendment, **Powers Reserved to the States**. "Powers not delegated to The United States by the Constitution, nor prohibited by it to the states, are reserved to the states or to the people. This is sometimes called implied powers. What does this really mean?

Delegation is to give a task to somebody else with responsibility on your behalf. That leaves it open for interpretation. Who is to interpret the Constitution? The United States Supreme Court is and is there a record of South Carolina or any one else investigating using this to try and solve this issue? After the Civil War, Texas did look into this in *Texas v. White* Supreme Court 1869; in that case, the court determined that the drafters intended the perpetuity of the Union to survive: "By the Articles of Confederation, the Union was solemnly declared to "be perpetual." And when these Articles were found to be inadequate to the exigencies of the country, the Constitution was ordained "to form a more perfect Union." It is difficult to convey the idea of indissoluble unity more clearly than by these words. **What can be indissoluble a Perpetual Union, if made more perfect, is not?"**

It looks like economically driven emotions led to bypassing law and turning a lost election into war.

Jefferson Davis spends much time talking about sectionalism in his book *Rise and Fall of the Confederacy*. He is also forthcoming about discussions in the U.S. Congress and he appears to put credence on what the congress says. With the election of Lincoln and the change in power by the admission of California as a free state, it looks like Davis and the South were not interested in what the new and seceding congresses would do. **Thus his arguments fall into the abyss of when my stance is winning I will use these arguments of congress but when my stance might lose I can't or won't wait to let the other side use the same arguments of congress.**

Davis had had some success in Congress. He advocated purchasing from Mexico land to help make a southern coast to coast railway. In 1853 the Gadsden Purchase as it was known, happened. The Kansas-Nebraska act and the Dred Scott Supreme Court case in 1857 were considered victories for the South. Although considered legislative or judicial victories at the time, they were not political victories as they actually galvanized the Republican positions in the North. Several House seats changed parties as the Southern support not only reeled from Dred Scott and Bleeding Kansas but also from the book, *Uncle Tom's Cabin.* **A Southerner being in the White House or a Northerner with Southern beliefs being in the White House was not going to happen in 1860.**

Chapter 14   Comparing Constitutions

The documents are remarkably very similar. The biggest difference in the United States Constitution and the Confederate States of America's Constitution is the mentioning of slavery. In four areas, slavery is specifically mentioned in the Confederate Constitution but some state rights are actually more limited. Those state right losses in the Confederate Constitution are that a state can't establish who can vote, can't outlaw the owning of slaves, or trade freely with other states. The government has some spending regulations and a restriction such as: the Post Office is on its own after a couple of years; some other innovative ideas such as line item veto and term limits; legislative bills can not have riders; and protective tariffs are forbidden. There were also four little quirks in the wording that could lead to states issuing their own money, taking away their voting right in congress as long as they allow representation, term limit for President but not for Vice President, and the government can extradite one for state crimes but not for a national crime. I have spent considerable time trying to prove that the Secession and creation of the Confederate States of America was not a 'State's Rights issue. **It was an economic issue involving the expansion of slavery.**

The North was not innocent in this whole affair. The issue of breaking up of the Union was raised by Abolitionist, William Lloyd Garrison who said, "No union with slave holders". President James Buchannan was called a Doughface by the North, meaning he was a Northerner with Southern principles. He was angry at the Abolitionists as he was working with some groups on a gradual end to slavery. The Abolitionists got everyone all stirred up. There had been some unfair tariffs that helped industry and hurt agriculture; with the North having more industry and the South more agriculture, these tariffs were unfair. Thus short of war, someone had to come up with an idea that would compensate the southern slave owners at the same time replacing their workers. At the end of the Civil War, Southern wealth was decreased by 60% and ¼ of their white men killed.[29]Looking back on it now, financially speaking, **everyone-but especially the South-would have been way ahead to have bought the slaves and freed them, than fight such a terribly destructive Civil War.**

Chapter 15 Seven ways the South could have won the Civil War.

1. Sticking to the plan to fight a defensive war. Lee ventured into northern territory twice, only to have two great battle losses. Antietam & Gettysburg were big victories for the North. (The battles were considered a victory for the North because the outcome was retreat to Virginia for Lee's army even though the battles had been close). **Gettysburg came on the same day as Grants victory at Vicksburg.**

2. After Antietam, the South had two major victories at Fredericksburg and Chancellorsville. But the battle of Antietam came at the very time that Great Britain was deciding whether or not to support the South. Great Britain had grown almost addicted to southern cotton. The victory by the North (again it might have been a victory of just stopping the Confederates), gave Lincoln the victory he needed to issue his Emancipation Proclamation. Recently, laws had been passed ending slavery in Great Britain. No matter how addicted Great Britain was to southern cotton, **it could not overcome the anti-slavery movement there.**

3. Several Confederate leaders also thought that Maryland would join the South if it could. In fact, the first casualties of the war were Union soldiers marching to Washington through Baltimore Maryland. Without Union troops forcing Marylanders to stay in the Union, most would flock to the Confederate Cause it was argued. However, when some possible recruits from Maryland showed up at Lee's camp and noticed how poorly dressed and equipped the confederate soldier was, most Marylanders returned home. The South didn't win as many hearts or minds in Maryland as they thought they would. **Twice**

as many Marylanders actually fought for the Union as for the Confederacy.[30]

4. Southern railroads were very underdeveloped. The different widths of the rail lines greatly hampered rapid transport of troop and supplies. Each state allowed the railroads to develop on their own. Many railroads just ran to the river docks so that cotton and tobacco could be brought there and shipped by river boats down to New Orleans. Most of the South's tracks ran east to West. With the North gaining control over the river traffic, those railroads became basically obsolete.[31] The war supplies that the Western Confederacy could have sent east, like cattle from Texas were stopped with the losses of Vicksburg, New Orleans and the rest of the Mississippi River. **Most of the North's tracks ran North and South allowing for rapid supply and troop movements to the front.**

5. If Lee had listened to Longstreet at Gettysburg and moved the battle closer to Washington D.C. his troops could have taken the high ground instead of stubbornly attacking the Federal positions that were already established on high ground. Union reinforcements were also close at hand to repel Pickett's charge at the moment the charge reached "The Angle". This is sometimes known as the "high water mark of the Confederacy". However; with the Union reinforcements so close, **the Union turned back the charge and decimated Pickett's Brigade.**

6. At the first battle of Bull Run, if the Rebel army could have been disciplined enough to effectively follow the retreating Union soldiers, Washington D.C., Abraham Lincoln and even the war may have been captured and ended. It has been stated that the Union forces ran back to Washington D.C. as fast as they could, throwing away their rifles and backpacks. Many Confederate forces stopped to pick up the equipment. This action underscores the basic problem of the Southern forces. Throughout the war, the Confederates suffered from lack of equipment or poor quality of equipment. **Lack of factories, funds, or the ability to trade plagued the South for the entire war.**

7. By not attacking Fort Sumter. This attack simply started the war. It was exciting to the people of Charleston and it made them feel good

in April of 1861, but they did not feel the same way in April of 1865. If the Confederates had not attacked the fort, then the onus of starting the war would have been on the Union. As the war dragged on, more Northerners would have been more disgruntled. Lincoln had not really done anything to the South even though most of the Federal property in the South had been seized except for a few forts in Florida and Fort Sumter in South Carolina. The attack and surrender brought about waves of patriotism in the North especially in New York City when Major Anderson, the former commander of Fort Sumter, brought the battered and torn flag that had flown over the fort during the attack, and flew it in New York City. It was like after Pearl Harbor or 911. Thousands of New York volunteers signed up. **Without the attack, would they have been so patriotic?**

Note: I don't include the tragic accidental death of Stonewall Jackson as a way of winning the war for the South. Jackson's example of standing firm helped the Confederates immensely in the early battles. It gave the Confederacy a super star whose conduct probably help prolonged the war by a couple of years. Even if Jackson would have lived, **the South still would have lost the war.**

I also don't include the belief of Jefferson Davis and a few others who felt that keeping a guerilla war going would help the South eventually to rise again. Robert E. Lee and General Johnston realized that the continued cost would not be worth the gain. The South had already lost too much. **Lee and Johnston showed the way.**

Jefferson Davis or whoever the leader of the Confederacy would have been had a monumental task. I don't feel that the blame some heap on Davis really makes a difference. With a staunch 'states' rights' type of government being forced to wage a war requiring very federal government type actions, **the confederate government was doomed from the beginning**.

I also dismiss the ideas of Confederate Senator William Oldham of Texas, who thought that the capitol in Richmond cost the South too much to defend and that it would have been better if the capital had been deeper into the south.[32] He also thought that the Southern leaders abandoned Southern ideals with conscription and militaralism and other war tactics. This included the poor effort to export and import through Mexico. I feel that although some of Oldham's ideas would have been helpful to the South, it still does not match the over-whelming assets of the North. In fact in his own writings, Oldham points out at the end of the war, the Southern people refused to stand up to the invading sorties by Union troops, especially cavalry when there were "plenty of able-bodied men around". What this actually shows is the successful results of total war waged by the North. Sherman's march to the sea and Grant's persistence wore down the spirit of the common people of the South. Southerners had been through tremendous hardships and had already suffered much and **there was just no hope after Lee's surrender**.

The "Cotton as King" presumption was a mistake by the South. Cotton may have been king in peace time but with the blockade of Southern ports, Great Britain expanded their cotton production in both India and Egypt where there was little chance of war interfering with delivery. With that choice available, it was cheaper and safer than going to war with the United States. A war with the United States, even if successful, would have only netted the British cotton supplier-again, only if they were successful, and **what would have been the cost of that success?**

Finally, I did not include ways that the North could have won the war sooner. That could be a book in itself. The North had numerous chances but failed to follow up due mainly to ineptness of their commanding generals. This led to major headaches for Lincoln and prolonged the war. A prime example of a chance not taken was immediately after the battle of Gettysburg. The Potomac River was swollen with recent rains and delayed Lee's retreat at the edge of the river.[33] He had nowhere to go and his army was demoralized, depleted, and stopped at a very poor defensive position, **but there was no attack by Union forces**.

Probably the number one way the war would have been shorter is if Robert E. Lee would have taken the Union Command that he was offered. That would have given the North the competent Commander they continually looked for, and prohibited the South from having **their best general**.

Chapter 16   Robert E. Lee's Decision

Lee had a very impressive pedigree and resume from the United States of America. He was a graduate of West Point (2nd in his class). He was Superintendant of West Point from 1852-1855. He was an Officer in the United States Army and fought in the Mexican War receiving three battlefield promotions as a Captain of Engineers. His father, Henry Light-Horse Lee, was an outstanding general in the American Revolutionary War. Two members of Lee's family tree signed the Declaration of Independence. His wife was the Great Grand Daughter of George Washington. His home, (Custis/Lee Mansion), overlooks the city of Washington D.C. **He was offered the command of all Union forces.**

Several reasons have been given as to why Lee gave all of that up to serve in the Confederate Army. Many of the Generals on both sides had higher political aspirations. Lee did not. Some historians think that Lee was upset that Lincoln did not try to solve things before Fort Sumter. His Father's second cousin probably wrote *Letters from a Federal Farmer,* as an answer to the Federalist Papers. Most of those arguments had been put to rest with the passage of the Bill of Rights and Robert E. Lee was not political. Lee did not like slavery nor did he rally to the southern cause. **I believe that Lee, very simply, loved his state of Virginia more than he did the United States.**

(Note: part of me still finds that incredulous. Lee had traveled extensively for a person of his time. With his background coupled with the fact that every morning he looked out at Washington D.C. just across the Potomac River from his plantation. With his beloved Virginia's capital of Richmond 100 miles away and he still chose Virginia!)? The North didn't like his decision and they made sure that win, lose, or draw, Lee would not be able to use his plantation again. The Union Army started burying soldiers on the property. **Today Lee's home and lands are known as Arlington National Cemetery.**

Chapter 17 Civil War

The Civil War is one of the most interesting and tragic periods of any country's history. Sectionalism turned into Nationalism almost immediately. The Rebs and the Yanks, the Blue and the Grey, the Stars and Stripes, and the Stars and Bars. Dixie and the Battle Hymn of the Republic, the Monitor and the Merrimac, Grant and Lee, all are well known opposites. The battles such as Bull Run, Chancellorsville, Fredericksburg, Antietam, Shiloh, Vicksburg, Gettysburg, Spotsylvania, Cold Harbor, the Wilderness, Appomattox Court House, Petersburg, and more will live on as great battles. The South, with all its heart, could not stand forever versus total war. Due to Sheridan in the Shenandoah Valley, Sherman's march to the sea, the naval blockade including the ironclad ships, the telegraph, the railroad, a national currency, the increasing population of the North due to immigration, the manufacturing of new and deadlier weapons, and even the Income Tax, **the South had no permanent answer but surrender.**

Some positives developments for mankind made during the Civil War were the major improvements in medicine and medical care. From medicines to Doctors, to Nurses, all made giant strides because of the need caused by the war. Doctors had very minimal training before the war. Gangrene, the cause of many amputations early in the war was largely reduced by the use of Bromide. Surgery techniques improved just from the vast number of amputations done. Improved Hospital design that separated patients into wards helping to stop the spread of some diseases. Cleanliness was one of the biggest realizations. Medical personnel came to be considered neutral on the battle field and therefore not to be shot at or captured. Clara Barton nursed on several battlefields, years later she established the Red Cross. Even the care of the deceased dramatically improved with embalming. Rare at the beginning of the war, it was common at the end. Abraham Lincoln's body went on a 14 cities tour after his assassination. **That would not have been possible without the new improvements in embalming.**

With so many farmers off fighting in the army of the North, one would think that agricultural production declined. Actually there was an increase in production, **probably helped by the 165,000 new reapers and other farm machinery bought by Northern farmers.**

Another positive development was the development of the game of Baseball. General Abner Doubleday is given credit for helping to spread the knowledge of how to play the game. Doubleday was the General who replaced Reynolds who had been killed on the first day of the Battle of Gettysburg. With so many young men in camp and with all their energy, some recreation was needed to help relieve the pressures of war. Whether Doubleday invented the game or not really doesn't matter. **The result was all those boys going home with the knowledge and love of playing and therefore; the game spread like wildfire.**

Besides the death and destruction I believe that there was another quasi-negative or positive depending on how you see the glass of water. Is it half full, or half empty? The same is true with Slavery. The Emancipation and the Constitutional Amendments ended hundreds of years of involuntary servitude but it served only to tease the African American community. African Americans fought in the Civil War and after the war some were elected to Congress, but lack of education and racial prejudice was hard to overcome. Soon Jim Crow Laws were in place and so was the KKK and the Supreme Court ruling of Plessey v. Ferguson saying "separate was equal." **True the African Americans were free after the war, but with sharecropping and Jury nullification, they probably had less protection than during slavery.** As painful as the process was, big steps had been taken but it was too slow.

Chapter 18   Reconstruction

All of these improvements pale compared to the damage inflicted on both sides. Since we are all Americans, the damage to both sides must be added together. With over 600,000 casualties after the war, reconstruction, as it was known, was not quick or without strife. Many in the North wanted to punish the South especially after the assassination of Abraham Lincoln. Many Southerners especially the ones further away from the fighting or the North were really not repentant, defeated people. [34]The end result was rule by Radical Republicans over President Andrew Johnson's vetos. Johnson, from Tennessee, survived impeachment by one vote. The 13th, 14th, and 15[th]amendments to the Constitution were passed. The 13th Amendment outlawed slavery. The 14th Amendment granted citizenship to all persons born in the United States and guaranteed all citizens "equal protection under the law." The 15th Amendment forbade any state to deny anyone the right to vote because of their race. One would erroneously think that just one amendment was needed to correct this injustice. **The fact that there are so many amendments shows how deeply the southern way of life was engrained in them and how hard it was for most southerners to grant equality.**

With so many of the former ruling class unable to vote, African Americans and radical Republicans were able to win the elections and hold office. The Freedmen's Bureau worked to help educate and employ blacks. Many of the white citizens could have been persuaded to accept the changes if things would have been better. With rampant corruption, very high taxes, and general chaos, many whites looked for other alternatives. **Many joined a radical white hate group called the Ku Klux Klan.**

This might seem to be the lowest point for the Confederacy but even at this low tide change is difficult. The tide of sectional pride gradually came back. The people who had been in power before the war wanted to change very little. Reforms were resisted on every street corner. People fought to regain the control that they had held for so long. One effective way was to continue the plantation economy through sharecropping. Most former slaves had no education and no where to go. Many just stayed on the very plantations that they had been on and did the work through a cruel but ingenuous system called sharecropping. Sharecropping was a way for the former slaves to do the work and share the crop with the land owner in the form of rent. Many poor white small farmers also fell into this same category. One catch was the equipment and seeds etc. usually belonged to the landowner who charged the workers rent. The rent always exceeded the profits so the workers had to stay on the plantation. **They stayed, not as slaves but as people in debt who could not afford to move**.

Carpetbaggers and Scalawags, as most history students remember, are Post Civil War terms. Carpetbaggers, although not a complimentary term, is a descriptive term of people coming into an area with their belongings in a bag made out of carpet. A scalawag on the other hand, is a derogatory term. One way to look at "scalawags" is as a rascal, another was a small, scruffy horse. Neither of these ways is very complimentary. But how should we look at or think of these individuals? For whatever reason, these people did not want to break away from the United States while everyone around them formed the Confederacy and fought against the United States. Some people might call them heroes and patriots but to people in the South they were traitors. **Why is it that most History texts use the same terms that former Confederates would use, Scalawags?**[35]

The high water mark of the Confederacy after the Civil War would be the disputed election in 1876 of Republican Rutherford B. Hayes and Samuel J. Tilden for President. Some Historians say that the North finally got tired of trying to change the sentiment of the South and decided to take care of their own affairs. While there may be some merit in that, I feel it is something much viler, almost evil in the backroom deal for the office of President. Tilden had over 250,000 more votes but was one short in the Electoral College.[36] Several disputed votes in the Electoral College were in South Carolina, Florida and Louisiana, states that were still controlled by Republicans. A commission was finally formed made up primarily of Republicans and they awarded the presidency to Hayes. Tilden could have still protested the ruling but Hayes made a backroom deal to pull the troops out of the South. **The Presidency, in exchange for the end of Reconstruction, what a deal.**

The Republican hold on Southern states was already beginning to wane as in 1872 former Confederates were again allowed to vote. Many voters were disgruntled with the corruption that had marked Grant's Administration and the intimidation of African American voters which was on the rise. With the army gone, the South retaliated with what are known as Jim Crow laws. These are many actions to basically enforce racial segregation and prevent African Americans from voting. The South also started voting solidly for the Democratic Party. By voting solidly as a block and restricting the vote of the opposition, the former confederate states were able to pass laws institutionalizing segregation. These laws or rules were not just legally enforced. There were lots of intimidations of African Americans by groups such as the KKK. The social fabric was constructed to keep African Americans 'in their place'. Even the Supreme Court of the United States contributed to this segregation. In 1896 in the case of *Plessey v. Ferguson*, the court ruled that "separate was equal." This was the law of the land for more than 50 years until the 1954 Supreme Court ruling in *Brown v. the Board of Education of Topeka, Kansas*. Many Southerners were openly very racist as Senator Ben Tillman of South Carolina stated, "The Democratic Party has only one plank, namely, this is a white man's country and white men must govern it." [37] One of the most ironic moments was a speech by President Woodrow Wilson at Gettysburg, Pennsylvania on July 4th, 1913. Wilson, a southerner was moving to segregate federal offices. **One reporter in attendance wondered aloud which side had really won at Gettysburg.**

Chapter 19 KKK

Our intolerance may be traced back to England between 1500-1600's. When England conquered Ireland, laws were passed against intermarrying or even wearing their clothes to look like them. One of the few exceptions to this was the marriage of Pocahontas to John Rolfe. The Spanish on the other hand did not have the restrictions and today a combination between Spaniards and American Indian is called mestizos and is more commonly called Mexican. Most of our early immigrants were British and they came with this attitude toward others of exclusion. The start of this prejudice might not have been known nor understood. It just was "the way it always had been." **People tend to continue to do things till someone with some gumption stands up and says why.**

I have debated how much to include about the KKK. Many of the members of that group were believers in State's Rights and limited Federal Government. Most were members from the South who had sympathetic feelings for the Old Confederacy. Many members felt that by force of the Federal Government, through use of Union soldiers, African Americans were given many more opportunities and many of those opportunities had come at the expense of whites. Therefore: through force of their own, they felt that they could intimidate African Americans from competing for those opportunities. I don't want the idea of smaller government, more local control, less taxation and other confederation issues to be hijacked by race-hating, restrictive religion and bullies who wear sheets. **The confederation ideal should never be confused with racism.**

The KKK had two active phases. One started up soon after the Civil War. Confederate General Forrest Bedford was one of its leaders. African Americans were physically intimidated and many were kept from voting out of fear. Congress did authorize the Enforcement Act of 1871 allowing Federal troops to be used in Klan areas, but in 1872 the

Amnesty Act was passed allowing former Confederates to vote again. **They voted against the Republicans and White Supremacy was reestablished in the South; the need for the Klan diminished.**

After WWI, the Klan again rises by combining anti race, religion and isolationism and anti- communism forces. In 1924 they had a membership approaching 4.5 million. They were opposed to Catholics, Jews, Unions, foreign born immigrants and even saloons in addition to their intimidation of African Americans. **The Great Depression and WWII changed the country in many ways and lessoned the influence of such hate groups.**

Still, many people clouded the issue with race and States' Rights and they then provided the Federalism side momentum when Southern state by Southern state was seen denying citizens their civil rights. Many local and state court juries practiced **jury nullification**. That is, if a person of your peer group does something illegal but it conforms with current social mores of your peer group, their actions, no matter how egregious, would be exonerated instead of condemned. Most of the convictions in Southern Civil Rights cases of the 1960's were of violation of someone's civil rights. These convictions happened after local courts had found the defendants not guilty even though there had been a preponderance of proof. **With the whole nation watching on television, the South had not yet learned how to use that medium to their favor.**

A new group of lawyers were coming on the scene and they rigorously pursued action against the Klan. Fourteen years after the bombing at the Sixteenth Street Baptist Church, the murderer of the four girls was convicted in 1977. It took until 2002 for his Klan partners to be convicted. In 1981, a 19 year old African American, Michael Donald was kidnapped and then lynched. Through the course of his trial, the Klan was implicated and in 1997 his murderer was executed. **It was the first time in over 80 years that a guilty white man was executed for a lynching of a black man.** In 1987 the Southern Poverty Law Center on behalf of the victim's family sued the National Organization of the Ku Klux Klan called the United Klans of America and won. The financial award wiped out the organization and their numbers. They were forced to give over their national headquarters building and property to the victim's family. [38]The few remaining believers' response was to diversitize into smaller independent groups. Today there is evidence **that some of these groups have become small paramilitary groups.**

Chapter 20 The Politically Progressive Era

Many needed reforms started near the end of the 19th century. A group of writers wrote about corruption in government and abuses in business. They were called 'Muckrakers'. Many groups were formed to begin to help the poor such as the Salvation Army and the YMCA which serve as good examples of the Social Gospel movement. The Women's Christian Temperance union led by Frances Willard had 245,000 members. Carry Nation would carry an axe around to smash bottles of liquor. Labor was pushing for an eight hour work day and a forty hour work week. **But the reforms most pertinent to our discussions came in the area of politics.**

State reforms led by Wisconsin Governor Robert M. La Follett and reforms in cities where new types of leaderships were tried, are examples of political reform on the state and local levels. City managers or city commissions worked in some cities after major disasters. Mayors struggled with price gouging until some cities took over the utilities. **Today, we just naturally think of municipal utilities as an everyday term.**

While municipal utilities are a good improvement, it adds to government and pushes towards more government and federalism. In this, as in many cases, it was a good thing. The progressive movement pushed in the other direction also by broadening the electorate. The women suffrage movement, led by Susan B. Anthony, made big progress, although at the same time Jim Crow laws were stifling the African American voting rights in the South. **The Progressive movement did make improvement in reducing government control by big business or political machines.**

The Australian secret ballot was introduced and adopted in many states. No one now knows who you vote for. Senators are now directly elected by people instead of by state legislatures. Minnesota became the first state to have a mandatory primary in 1899. Now people, not party bosses, have more say as to whom candidates will be. Three important powers were taken back by the people in some states. **Initiative** is a way the people can introduce legislation on the ballot if the legislature can't or won't bring it up to a vote. On some complicated social issues the legislatures would just as soon let the public vote on it and that is called a **referendum**. In some states, if after a time the people really don't like either the ethical behavior of the politician or the political actions taken by the politician, they can call for a **recall** vote. That is, to remove that person from that office and hold an election to replace him.

Recall was mentioned in the Articles of Confederation and Perpetual Union and in Ancient Greece. Recall votes have only been successful a few times. 18 states have recall for Governor; in 2003 Grey Davis of California was recalled over budget battles and Arnold Schwarzenegger was then elected. In 1921 the people of North Dakota recalled Lynn Frazier over use of some state-owned industries. In 1967, Senator Frank Church from Idaho was not subject to recall as **the courts ruled that federal officials are not subject to the states rules.**

While not shrinking the size of government, these reforms establish some parameters around government and greatly expand the people's political influence. They are steps taken toward direct democracy. While these reforms were needed and most were useful, direct democracy has some serious draw backs. It's not that people couldn't do it but it is that most of us don't have time to do it. We wouldn't want anyone voting on legislation that they haven't investigated. Also, our Founding Fathers were smart enough to include a buffer zone from mob rule. **In direct democracy, there are no checks and balances and no time delays that allow cooler heads to prevail.**

Chapter 21   When does the pendulum of sentiment swing between Federalism or Confederation?

During the Revolutionary War, the Colonies figured out that they needed a unified commander. They found a good one in George Washington. The Colonies didn't always properly outfit the army. You've heard the stories from Valley Forge-bloody footprints in the snow because of no shoes-and in Morristown, two years later it actually had been even colder and a much worse winter encampment. All throughout the war, **the dichotomy of national control at variance with local support began with the earliest stages of the American life even under life threatening circumstances.**

All through our history in times of crisis, such as in December 7, 1941, and September 11, 2001, or during the economic crisis in the 1930's, the pendulum swings naturally to Federalism. **In absence of a federal emergency or in a time of perceived high taxes, deficit spending, or scandals, the pendulum swings back towards states' rights and smaller government.**

Like all major organizations, our government is sometimes rocked with scandals. These scandals usually have something to do with money or sex. The Teapot Dome Oil scandal and President Bill Clinton's 'intern problem,' would be good examples. I am not going to spent time on the sex scandals of Presidents, Senators, Governors, or even golfers, just let it suffice that when it happens, it lowers the opinions of the voters of our public servants. **Power, over the centuries, has always been a very strong aphrodisiac.**

The Teapot Dome scandal happened under popular President Warren G. Harding in the twenties. Teapot Dome is the name of the rock formation in Wyoming where the oil fields were located. The scandal also included fields in California called the Elk Hills Reserves. Harding's reputation was tarnished by this scandal but only because it was one of his cabinet members, Albert B. Fall, Secretary of the Interior, who was involved. Harding died in 1923 while still in office and in the midst of the investigations. Fall, a former Republican Senator from New Mexico, wanted the U.S. to end the holding of certain oil reserves and let private oil companies operate on public land. With billions of dollars at stake, Fall was bribed by Harry Sinclair of Sinclair Oil and Edward Doheny of Pan American Oil to grant oil leases without having other bids. This was legal under the law of the times but what was illegal was taking 'loans' of over 4 million dollars of today's value. Fall got one year in jail and so did Sinclair. They still probably came out ahead, but the country remained in a small government mode. **The Supreme Court added some clout to Congress by establishing the right of Congress to force people to testimony in congressional hearings as a result of the whole Teapot Dome affair.**

Power can also be a temptation to scandal. Take the Watergate scandal of the 1970's. Richard Nixon was President. He had fought very hard to get there. He fought hard to get on the ticket with Dwight D. Eisenhower by being hard on Communism. One time his reputation was on the line and he gave his famous "Checkers" speech. Accused of getting some gifts inappropriately, Nixon in a televised speech said that he would not give back his little girls' dog "Checkers." That speech brought him to the political forefront. He lost in a very close election to John F. Kennedy in 1960. His loss, some claim, was due in part to a televised debate in which Kennedy looked calmer and more Presidential and Nixon more nervous. Part of that look has been credited to the **lack of television make up that Nixon decided not wear.**

After Lyndon Johnson's announcement that he would not run in 1968, and all the turmoil surrounding the assassinations of Martin Luther King Jr. and Robert Kennedy, and the race riots, the Vietnam War protests, the counter-culture movement, Nixon was elected. The country had wanted someone who would take the country back to law and order. The silent majority elected Nixon. As President, he eventually ended the use of American soldiers in the Vietnam War and had a **surprise visit to Communist China setting up trade opportunities**.

So far this is a great story of a great man, but Nixon had a darker side. He was paranoid. He had a list of people who had been against him. He felt people never did like him as much. JFK was accused of womanizing but everybody loved him. Nixon, a loyal family man, felt that nobody really liked him. Nixon was probably right, but he was President and he would make sure that he would be reelected. J. Edgar Hoover of the FBI had everyone investigated including Martin Luther King Jr. but Nixon needed more. A group called CRP, [which also happen to be my initials so I'll use CReeP], (committee to reelect the president) managed to get some guys to break into the office of the National Democratic Party's Headquarters. **The office was in a hotel in Georgetown near the old Chesapeake and Ohio Canal's lock--the hotel's name was Watergate!**

Watergate has its own fascinating story with intrigue, deceit, an undercover mole, denials, and the tapes. The story is brought out by two young reporters for the Washington Post who get stuck investigating a nothing story. Bob Woodward and Carl Bernstein kept getting stonewalled by officials while investigating this nothing of a story. They sensed correctly that there must be something more to the story and they were right. They tell the story better in their books but my take on the whole **Watergate scandal is that this was the most dangerous scandal in our history.**

The purpose of the Watergate break-in was to gather information on the campaign strategies of the Democrats. With this information, they could use it to sabotage the Democrat's campaign, thus insuring Nixon's reelection. They had done some dirty tricks before against Edmund Muskie in the New Hampshire primary. This is dangerous because they are trying to take away Americans' right to vote. They tried national disenfranchisement. They, the committee to reelect the President, knew more than all of the rest of us--they were trying to choose instead of us. Besides being so very wrong, it was just plain stupid. The Democrats were so divided that they couldn't even mount a competitive race, and they didn't. **Nixon and his paranoia, along with his buddies, accomplished what no political party could do. That was to force Nixon, facing sure impeachment by the house and conviction by the Senate, to resign.**

On August 9th 1974, The United States of American had its first non elected President, Gerald R. Ford. Ford had replaced Nixon's Vice

President, Spiro Agnew who had not seen fit to pay his taxes. Fortunately for the country, Ford was a good replacement in many ways. **The result of all this turmoil was the election of a political outsider, Jimmy Carter, and the country took a step back from a strong President and Federalism towards Confederation.**

Carter's inability to successfully handle the Iran hostage crisis and the Iranian Islamic Revolution led the pendulum to swing back to a strong President. **Even though Ronald Reagan is touted as the "conservative standard bearer," many of his actions were very federalist.**

This swinging pendulum can be fickle and complicated. In 2010, President Obama came under criticism for the bailouts of Wall Street, and the Auto Industry. He had been called a Socialist and worse for his bailouts and Health Care Program. Calls from groups like the Tea Party and the far right Republicans were very critical of too much government involvement. Then BP (formerly British Petroleum) had the disastrous offshore oil well explosion and resultant leak and pollution of the southern shores. **Suddenly, our government was not too big. It was "not doing enough!" As though the government should know more than the Oil Industry, and the government should know how to stop a massive oil leak in over a mile deep water, even though it had never been tried before.**

So the government stepped in. To insure that more spills wouldn't happen, a drilling moratorium was mandated to investigate drilling companies' policies and procedures. **Now the government was too big and it should let the marketplace work.**

When the New York Mosque building debate was the hot news topic, the big question was where was the money coming from? They didn't want money from Islamic countries or terrorist groups to be used. Even though no money had actually been raised yet, it was a major talking point. The same people don't seem to have a problem with the new campaign rules allowing undisclosed contributions from corporations to be used. Some of that money maybe coming from overseas, we don't know. **Not only can the pendulum's swinging be fickle, it can also be hypocritical.**

After 2010 we can add what seems to be a new rule for the cause of a swinging pendulum but in reality, it is the oldest rule of all. The economy makes the pendulum move and the worse the economy is, the faster and further it swings. **Franklin Roosevelt won four terms as President after the Great Depression caused a swing. The state of the economy, more than anything else will determine Obama's fate in 2012.**

Chapter 22   Business and Labor

Much of the 20th century has been dominated by wars and depression, or so it seems. In actuality Big Business dominated. Big Business with big profits for owners and low wages, poor working conditions and long hours for the workers has been more dominant. Corporations, compared to individuals or family owned businesses or even limited partnerships routinely show lack of a heart. A corporation is not a person. This has led to tremendous wealth for the wealthy and unfortunately corruption. President Calvin Coolidge who was nicknamed Silent Cal spoke up enough to expound the American philosophy when he said, **"The business of America, is Business!"**

The pendulum of political power based on states' rights confederation or big government federalism does not swing in a vacuum. That pendulum swings in a fluid of business. The size of business likes to compete with the size of government. Business likes little involvement or over-seeing by the government. Regulation hampers the growth of business. Unfortunately, lack of enforced regulation leads to wide spread abuses by business. **The interest of Big Business is usually not the interest of the American people.**

The size of government is not the only struggle going on. There is a never-ending struggle between Labor and Business. When the industrial revolution hit America, a revolutionary ideal was formed and put into practice by Francis Lowell of Massachusetts. The Lowell experiment was to build a complete factory town. His factory was a textile factory and the labor could be done by women. Young girls would come and live in worker dorms complete with a house mother and with a school and church nearby. They hired the women because they could pay them half of what it would cost to pay a man.[39]Because of the size of the machines, little fingers were needed. Routinely children around the age of 7 worked for 12 hours a day for 6 days a week. Child labor laws would have to be passed because even though the Lowell experiment started out with great promise and hope, competition forced business to push its workers into more production. **Safety, higher wages, better benefits, shorter hours, health care insurance and a retirement plan weren't even on the horizon for business.**

In 1836, Massachusetts passed a law limiting children under 15 from working unless they had attended school. That was only the beginning. Facing the Laisse faire (hands off) theory of non government intervention into business, workers finally took things into their own hands. The "Molly McGuire's" Pennsylvania miners took to violence. Eventually the tone was set. Violence would meet violence. Between 1881 and 1905 there were 37,000 strikes. Most of the strikes were small and local but a few went national. In 1877 there was a railroad strike; actually there were several in different cities. Caused by the second pay cut after the economic 'Panic of 1873,' Federal troops had to be brought in to put down the riots. One of the railroad bosses had helped broker the election of Rutherford B. Hayes, who had not received as many votes as Samuel J. Tilden in the election of 1876, and that might have been a **factor in the Federal troops being sent in**.

On May 1st, 1886, all over the country, workers went on strike for the 8 hour work day. On May 3rd, while strikers were outside of the McCormick Harvesting Machine Company near Chicago, there was violence and two strikers were killed by police. The strikers planned another rally on May 4th at Haymarket Square. The rally was peaceable until the very end. With the police moving the crowd to go home, a pipe bomb was thrown at the police. One policeman was killed and others injured, but in the mayhem that followed, police opened fire on the crowd. Many people were wounded including several police due to friendly fire. 8 police and 4 strikers were killed. Hysteria followed the trial and 8 strike leaders were condemned to be hung. After appeals and a suicide, four were hung. 6 years later, the Governor of Illinois, John Altgeld ruled them all innocent. **Almost all of the accused were German immigrants.**

In 1890, the Sherman Anti Trust Act was passed. It meant to ensure competition in the work place but the first application was in 1894 and the Pullman train strike. After the economic downturn of 1893, Pullman lowered wages for the workers but kept high rent on houses in the company town of Pullman. When they went on strike, other railway workers refused to handle Pullman cars. Soon nationwide rail movement came to a stand still. President Grover Cleveland called on 12,000 Federal troops to put down the strike. Illinois Governor Altgeld was so angry at Cleveland that he blocked Cleveland's renomination as president. Eugene V. Debs was the leader of the striking union and he was placed on trial. He was defended by the famous Clarence Darrow of the more famous Scopes 'monkey' trial. Debs got 6 months on a technicality. While in jail, Debs read up on socialism and communism. After his release, he **ran for President as a Socialist five times, gathering as many as 900,000 votes in two of those elections.**

Lobbyists are nothing new to Washington. Limiting influence by outside special interest groups has been a problem for a long time, and has survived numerous attempts at legislative controls. In his picture entitled "Bosses of the Senate" Joseph Keppler tried to capture the spirit of perceived control of politics by big business. It appeared in *Puck* on January 23, 1889. The motto on the wall of the Senate Chamber said, "This is the Senate of the Monopolist, by the Monopolist, and for the Monopolist." The door marked "public" is locked and bolted. Heavy, top-hatted men of different Trusts stand in the back row dominating the Senators. The current issue is political ads paid for by a group some with the innoxious name of 'Citizens for a better tomorrow' for example. In reality, they are a business that can benefit by passing or rejecting certain legislation. We don't know who these 'Citizens' are or why they are taking their stand. They are trying to influence us by their ads but keeping us in the dark about their real identity. **I feel that if this is the type of misleading information that we don't allow to be used in advertisements of products, why do we allow it for the more important issue of politics?**

By 1900 wealth was concentrated in the hands of a few robber barons. These self made men were very wealthy. Of men like John D. Rockefeller, J.P. Morgan, Andrew Carnegie, John Jacob Astor, Cornelius Vanderbilt, James Duke, and Leland Stanford, it was said that they owned 99% of the wealth but had only 1% of the population. Robber Barons is a term that Labor might use. They might say that the vast amounts of wealth gathered by these men were obtained by gleaming profits, by skimming on wages and allowing unsafe working conditions. **The term 'Robber Barons' was used during the Great Depression by**

Mathew Josephson[40] in his 1934 book describing big industrialists at a time when big business wasn't very popular.

Business on the other hand, might point out that these industrialists by hard work and some ingenious foresight created wealth and jobs. The adaptation of Darwin's Theory of Evolution took on a sociological term called Social Darwinism. It was a belief that superior people won the war on poverty and wealth is the medal of evolution. An example is J.P. Morgan, who is credited with creating U.S. Steel and General Electric, also came to the country's aid by helping to finance the recovery in the Panic of 1893 and again in 1907. The latter led to the development of the Federal Reserve System. If you look at just their last names, one might recognize them for something else. Duke University, Stanford University, Vanderbilt University, Carnegie Hall, Carnegie Libraries, Rockefeller Center, University of Chicago, various museums, just to name a few of the many endowments and donations made by these industrialists shows their other side. **Many of the so called "Robber Barons" became great Philanthropists**.

In 1914 the Clayton Anti-trust Act was passed and that was a big boom for labor. It said that Unions were not an impediment to business and federal injunctions could not be used against them. Impatient with the AFL (American Federation of Labor) A new union was started. The Congress of Industrial Organizations was led by a fiery leader named John L. Lewis. **In 1938 The Fair Labor Standards Act finally made it a 40 hour work week with 40 cents per hour as a minimum wage.**

In 1947, over President Truman's veto, the Taft –Hartley Act was put into law. It allows for an open shop or a right to work and 60 day notice of a strike. This act was a law that favored business over labor. The President was authorized to intervene if a strike could hurt or create a national emergency. **Labor verses Business has been a long struggle**.

It would be great to have one's political party's motto as **Fiscal responsibity with regulation**. Business has always had the ability of pushing hard for profit and sometimes taking the short cuts along the way. Regulation is a needed necessity. Enforcement of regulations is a needed necessity. Just look at the financial problems of 2008 and 2009. This isn't new for the market either as we can just look back at the stock market crash on October 29, 1929, a day that is known as "Black Tuesday." And there are other examples in dealing with safety in the work place. **A great example of this need is the Triangle Shirtwaist Factory fire in 1911**.

The Triangle Shirtwaist Company was a business that employed mainly new immigrant labor in the making of clothes. It was located on the upper floors of the Asch building in New York City. Most of the workers were poor, young, Italian and Jewish girls, some recent immigrants or the daughters of immigrants. Some evidence suggest that because these girls would sometimes try to sneak out (steal) some shirts by hiding them on their body or even in their hair, the company would make the girls leave by using only one door so that they could inspect them for theft.[41] The company would lock the other doors. As fate would have it, near closing time on Saturday, March 25, 1911, with the garbage bins and the floor full of trimmings of very flammable material, a fire started. Even though attempts were made to put out the fire, it rapidly spread causing a myriad of preexisting problems to become catastrophic. **These would cost the lives of 146 workers.**

As horrible as the resultant deaths were, this fire came at a crucial time in our history. Labor unions were on the rise not only in the United States but also in the world. Socialism was looked on as an adjustment to Capitalism. There had been labor strikes calling for better wages and working conditions even by the workers at the Shirtwaist Factory. The owners were trying to follow the capitalist plan of making as much money as possible for themselves. With no shortage of new labor, owners would try to replace workers with new ones. This situation was repeating itself in many cities in the United States and also in the major cities of the industrialized world. This led to the escalation of violence. It was a dangerous time also overseas as violence erupted to overthrow the Tsar in Russia, creating the Soviet Union. Soviet is a term meaning workers. Karl Marx in his Communist Manifesto called on "Workers of the World unite." **Maybe in some small way, the reforms instituted after the Triangle Shirtwaist fire, prevented a workers' revolution here.**

One of the spectators watching the fire was a young reformer named Frances Perkins. She, along with all of the witnesses, was appalled at the sight of young girls jumping out of the building to their deaths on the sidewalks below. Their choice was to burn in the building or jump. Perkins would never forget it. She set out on a mission to reform and she took that reform years later to the New Deal. In fact, it has been said that this was the beginning of the New Deal. **Frances Perkins became**

the first woman in a presidential cabinet position when she became the Secretary of Labor.

Besides Perkins, Al Smith who became Governor of New York; Robert Wagner who became a Senator from New York; Samuel Gompers, the leader of the American Federation of Labor; and others worked on a commission to set up reforms. As a result we have many improvements in safety in the work place. Next time you are in a public building, or a private workplace, look around for fire safety items. Fire exits clear and marked clearly, fire extinguishers readily available, doors that open outwards, a sprinkler system required in higher buildings are some of the more obvious reforms. Fire Departments have a Fire Prevention Mandate and give training and information to the public. Other reforms such as written documents showing a fire prevention plan and the training in personnel might not be so obvious **but are required by OSHA.**

The Occupational Safety and Health Act was signed into law in 1970 by Richard Nixon. OSHA as it is known is just the latest in government restrictions on businesses for the protection of American workers and the public in general. After the Triangle fire, New York State began to use the recommendations of the committee and created protective legislation. This first in the country legislation forced other states to adopt safety laws. Robert Wagner took these ideas to the U.S. Senate to help make national laws, especially the **National Labor Relations Act.**

It is ironic that 5 years after the book *The Jungle* by Upton Sinclair, describing the horrible conditions in the Chicago meat packing industry, the work place was still unsafe. Ironic that Frances Perkins saw the fire at Triangle. Ironic that after all these new regulations, on the 79th anniversary of the Triangle Shirtwaist Fire, the Happy Land Social Club burned in the Bronx. 87 people died, most of who were customers. There was no sprinkler system, no fire alarm, only one exit as the other doors were locked and there were iron bars on the windows to keep people from breaking in. As ironic as that might seem, the Asch building is still being used today. **Students of New York University can look out the same windows the young victims leapt from on that fateful day back in 1911.**

Business and Labor are going to continuously struggle. When benefits, wages and taxes reach a point of no return on investment, business will find a way to cut expenses. With insurance expenses on the rise, businesses cut labor. It was cheaper to hire two part time employees and not have to pay their insurance than to hire one employee. Businesswise that works and more people are employed but the ½ time employee still needs insurance and they either buy in and pay high premiums since they are not in a pool or they simply go without. If you don't have insurance coverage you are less likely to get preventative medical care and then are more likely to have to get the more expensive emergency care when you are sick. **This problem affects all of us as some people in this group don't pay their hospital bills therefore we have to make up the difference.** The health care bill is supposed to put everyone in a pool to make the cost less for everyone. That remains to be seen.

Business has also invested in more machines to replace human workers. Initial expense, maintenance and flexibility are major concerns with robotics but they are making dramatic improvements. Think of their use in bomb detection and the use of drones in the military. All of those developments are saving lives. Accelerating since the 1990's, outsourcing labor has become big business's new weapon. A couple of years ago I had trouble with my computer. I called the company and was given a technician to talk to over the phone. He was a big help but I found out that he was <u>in</u> India. That has become so commonplace that there is even **a sitcom of an outsourcing firm on T.V.**

Labor's continuous demands for wage and benefits increases have led to a very high standard of living. To maintain that life style we need a certain amount of money. It is sometimes more cost effective to move the plant to a third world country or just to contract for products to be made somewhere else, somewhere where the costs are dramatically less. **Is it really a wonder why China's economy is growing?**

In a twist of fate, big labor unions have become big businesses. They manage huge retirement funds where it is in the workers' best interest that their company makes money.

We still face monumental problems even though we avoided the disaster of "too big to fail" companies. Look what happened when the giant oil company Enron dissolved. Many people had their investments wiped out but more lost their retirement. What is going to be the solution to our labor problems? We have fundamentally changed since WWII when we manufactured everything. During the American

Revolution and War of 1812 protective tariffs worked to improve our manufacturing as we were at war with the usual supplier. The tariffs were a sore spot with the South, and they were a leading cause for the Civil War. Protective tariffs were tried again with the passage of the Smoot-Hawley Act of 1930. It is considered the major cause of the deepness of the Great Depression. Some say that we were able to stop the spread of Communism in Europe by the Marshall plan. Today the political waters are not ripe for another bailout plan anytime in the foreseeable future. We just experienced an economically driven election. Never in our History have we faced more competition especially from huge collective areas. Brazil, India, China, South Korea, Japan, Thailand, Russia, and the European Union are all major competitors. **We still have lots of American ingenuity and Green just might be the color to paint it.**

Chapter 23   First half of the 20th Century

For most of the early 20th Century, Federalism dominates with WWI, the Great Depression and FDR's New Deal solutions. But before the War there was probably our most vibrant and energetic and principled citizen and he 'charged' his way into the White House. His name was Teddy Roosevelt. Having asthma as a child, he forced himself outside. He earned his fame in the 'Rough Riders' famous charge up San Juan Hill in Cuba during the Spanish American War. He had helped organize the Rough Riders and the charge made him a hero. Actually, the African American Buffalo Soldiers of the 10th Calvary beat them to the top according to John J. "Black Jack" Pershing. In WWI Pershing would become our only living General to be named General of the Armies.

Theodore Roosevelt and Rough Riders on San Juan Hill after their charge. There were two pictures of this event. Of the two, this one is a better picture. Here you can see that it has been cropped and Roosevelt and the flag are posed and used as the central focus. In the first uncropped version, one can see the 3rd U.S. Calvary on the left and the African American Buffalo Soldiers of the 10th Calvary on the right. In 1898, with yellow journalism at its height, why would the truth get in the way?

In a transportation snafu, most of the horses didn't make it. It is odd seeing the Calvary charge on foot.

The painting by Fredrick Remington also shows the charge that went up Kettle Hill led by Roosevelt. It was the picture and story promoting Roosevelt that made it into the papers and a hero was made. As it was, we had around 15,000 men to the Spanish 800. With 1500 casualties it was still a brave charge for all who made it. A 600 man counterattack by another Spanish unit was stopped by one Gatling gun inflicting 540 casualties on the Spanish. That attack was a prelude to machinegun warfare in WWI.

Theodore Roosevelt went on to become Governor of New York and soon Vice President. President William McKinley was assassinated and at age 42, Roosevelt was President. He liked to use the presidency as a 'bully pulpit' where he could espouse his vision of America. His foreign policy was summed up by "Speak softly but carry a big stick". In 1906 he brokered a peace treaty between Japan and Russia. **He loved the outdoors and his actions made him truly the most deserved person to be carved on Mount Rushmore.**

While hunting one time he rescued a little bear. Soon an enterprising businessman had started to make little stuffed bears. **They still are called 'Teddy' to this day, all in his honor.**

Teddy Roosevelt did many things to promote the general welfare, they were things he called the 'Square Deal.' From creating National Parks to regulating the meat packing industry in Chicago, to trust busting

(44 cases), Pure Food and Drug Act, Teddy Roosevelt actually became a huge federalist. He threatened to take over the mines during the Coal Strike of 1902. Coal in those days was the number one home heating source. **After that crisis, The Federal Government was expected to intervene when something threatened the publics' well being.** He invited Booker T. Washington to dinner at the White House. That might not seem like much but in his day; **he was severely criticized for having an African American leader in the White House. His enlarging of the fleet and then creating the whole climate around the construction of the Panama Canal screams of Federalism.**

His protégé, William Howard Taft continued on with 75 antitrust actions. Democrat Woodrow Wilson continued the trend with the Federal Reserve Act, Federal Trade Commission, the Clayton Antitrust Act, and the first progressive income tax. Wilson in retrospect, looks like he brought some of his racial views from Virginia but WWI would cast Wilson onto the world stage along with his 14 point plan and his **"War to end all wars."**

World War One like all wars requires centralized governmental control. In May of 1917, The Selective Service Act was passed, and over 3 million Americans were drafted. The War Industries Board was established and by spreading Henry Ford's ideas of assembly line production techniques, production improved by 20%. Other regulatory agencies included the Railroad Administration and the Fuel Administration. Fuel was rationed and people had gasless Sundays and lightness nights to do their part. Ben Franklin had proposed a fuel saving idea back in the 1770's and in March of 1918 it was tried and worked so well that we continue to use it today. (**'Daylight Savings Time'**)

Profits soared but prices also rose and there were many resultant labor disputes. A National War Labor Board was established and ordered workers to "work or fight," insinuating that failure to work would cost you your draft deferment. The board also improved factories by insisting on an 8 hour day, no child labor, and better safety conditions.[42]Herbert Hoover was placed at the head of the Food Administration and established "wheat-less" days and "pork-less" days, and "Victory Gardens" were planted everywhere. **Food production for the war effort tripled as farmers planted 40 million more acres.**

To pay for the war effort a progressive income tax was established along with increased excise taxes on liquor and tobacco and luxury goods. **2/3 thirds of the money was borrowed through the sale of war bonds called, "Victory Loans, or Liberty Loans."**

One of the most interesting big government creations was a propaganda agency called the Committee on Public Information. As with most things, there are two sides to the story. The CPI wrote millions of pamphlets, posters, and speeches and some of them, while patriotic, incited anti-immigrant feelings especially towards new German immigrants. President Wilson warned that "tolerance" would be one of the first things to go. Everyday items such as food that had a German origin such as sauerkraut became 'liberty cabbage,' hamburgers became 'Salisbury steak' and German measles became 'liberty measles'. Songs written by famous composers like Bach, Mozart, Brahms and Beethoven were not played or sung. Many towns changed their names if it sounded German. German Americans lost their jobs and some were attacked. **This anti immigrant feeling grew to include all immigrants not just the German immigrants.**

As in John Adam's time, as he tried to prevent war by issuing the Alien and Sedition Acts of 1798, so in 1917, Congress passed the Espionage Act and later in May of 1918, the Sedition Act. Criticism of the war was not tolerated and unions striking for higher pay had their leaders jailed. After 9/11 the Patriot Act would be enacted by Congress. **Three different centuries and in time of war, our rights have been usurped because of fear.**

Anti-immigrant feelings emotionally are not very far from racial discrimination. Many African Americans began to migrate to the northern cities to escape southern prejudice and get jobs in the war plants of the North. Problems occurred in St. Louis over African Americans being used as strike breakers. 49 people were killed in the resulting riots. Tensions over new workers reached a peak in Chicago when a young African American swam from a 'Black' beach to a 'White' beach. The Whites threw rocks at him and he drowned. **Over 10,000 people were engaged in the resultant riots.**

Women also joined the work force. Even though they didn't receive equal pay, their support of the war effort helped get the 19th amendment passed, allowing women to vote.

With these last few paragraphs, it is easy to see that the expansion of government during wartime is massive and all inclusive. As always, after a war, Americans retract their out reaches and move towards isolationism. This shortsightedness is very pronounced by the system of checks and balances in our Constitution. Wilson was able to broker an end to the war by having a 14 Point Peace Plan. At the end of the war, the treaty that Wilson had great influence over needed to be ratified by the Senate. One of the points in the treaty was the creation of the League of Nations. The tide of isolationism had come in and Wilson went around the country pleading for his cause. It even cost him his health. **The U.S. Senate rejected the 14 point peace treaty and the final treaty was so punitive towards Germany that a mere 20 years later, America and the world would be embroiled in a far deadlier and in every way more expensive world war against Germany and her allies.**

Things didn't just settle down after the war either, with labor strikes and the 'red scare' phenomenon. After the fall of Russia to the communists, many people especially anti union supporters believed that the unions were full of socialists and communists and people who didn't believed in any government called anarchists. Many Americans believed that they held a threat to our way of life. The 'Red Scare' was viciously opposed by Attorney General Mitchell Palmer. Palmer appointed J. Edgar Hoover as his special assistant. American civil rights were forgotten and many foreign born agitators were deported. **Trials, warrants, legal consuls and similar abuses that we had complained about the British doing to us as colonists were done again to Americans by our own government to combat the supposed communist threat.**

Warren G. Harding had campaigned on returning the country to 'normalcy.' It was a difficult task as mass immigrations were flooding America. A quota system was established that was biased against Catholics and Jews. It was also very restrictive of Japanese immigration. The **Japanese were very angry about it as they had abided by the restrictions of 1907. Interestingly enough, there were that no restrictions on North Americans applied and one million Canadians and half that amount of Mexicans came to America**.

The flood of immigrants corresponded with a rise of anti-immigration groups; most noticeable was the KKK.

Harding had other problems as many in his administration got involved in political scandals. Most famous of these was the Teapot Dome Scandals. Just as these were starting to become known, Harding dies.

Republican Calvin Coolidge might be the poster child of confederation. He believed in letting the market forces work. He became president after the death of Warren G. Harding in 1923 and served as president until 1928. The roaring 20's were highlighted by low taxes, small federal government expenditures with the economy in high gear. He did not like regulation and believed in laissez-faire. He did support Afro-Americans and Catholics who were the targets of a resurgent KKK and signed legislation making American Indians citizens of the United States while retaining their tribal heritage. Although known as silent Cal (and he was) he did give a record 520 news conferences. **With no real crisis, government and our pendulum was allowed to swing towards confederation.**

One of the Great Humanitarians of the First World War era was Herbert Hoover. He is generally blamed for not doing much during the beginning of the Great Depression. But on closer inspection that is not the case. He believed that keeping wages high would be the key to recovery, this belief hurt him with his party as that favored labor instead of business. Hoover enacted many remedies and as one Franklin Roosevelt appointee admitted years later, the New Deal in many ways was a continuation of Hoover's ideas.[43] His Reconstruction Finance Corporation and Agricultural Market Act, Emergency Relief and Construction Act were examples of "New Deal" prototype Acts. He cut taxes, increased government spending but he gave money directly to the banks instead of to business. Hoover started such major work projects as the San Francisco Bay Bridge, Hoover Dam, the L.A. Aqueduct, **but his biggest mistake was in not vetoing the Smoot-Hawley Tariff of 1930.**

Passed by the Republican Congress, over 1000 leading economist warned of dire consequences, Hoover succumbed to party pressure and the economic results cost him his reputation. While initially the tariff brought in some revenue, the retaliatory tariffs placed on U.S. exports killed world wide trade and as a direct result caused the collapse of the huge Kredit-Anstalt bank in Austria. This triggered a world wide Depression. The congress followed that with the Revenue Act of 1932 which was the greatest tax hike in history. Instead of being a president that tried to get us out of the Great Depression, Hoover's legacy is in "Hoover flags" (pants pockets pulled inside out indicating no money) and "Hoovervilles", a term coined by a democratic strategist becoming synonymous with abject poverty. Hoover believed that the economy would recover if left to market forces and **although wages remained high, 28% of the population had no wages.**[44]

The people couldn't wait for prosperity.

(Just a note of interjection here as other governments have fallen in such desperate times such as these. The monarchy of Louis XVI of France and the beginning of the French Revolution; the more contemporary rise of Adolph Hitler and the Nazi Party in Germany; and the Communist Revolution against tsarist Russia in 1917; all have beginnings in bad economic times. People won't always wait for change. America, with all of our faults went to the ballot box instead.)

Franklin Roosevelt, promised to take care of the people till prosperity came. He had to come up with ideas to have people feed themselves and keep families together. The CCC or Civilian Conservation Corps was an army of men that worked hard to improve State Parks and Camps. These works jobs gave workers a job, and a paycheck. Most importantly the jobs gave the men the feeling of self worth. The New Deal consisted in bank reform and hundreds of ideas to help the people. The preamble of the Constitution does say to promote the general welfare but is this what they had in mind? Some of his plans could be called socialism.

Socialism, state ownership of certain industries is a help I gave the students to remember this. Some industry needs to be limited and owned for the good of the people. The United States Post Office is a good example, even though there is competition for delivery of packages, it makes more sense to have just one mail carrier. In cities where power lines and gas lines have been placed underground, most cities now own the utilities company. That makes sense because if one company needs to dig for a gas main problem, that company doesn't have to worry about digging into another company's gas main by mistake. **Some government ownership is just practical**.

Many people had no financial reserves to survive and most had used up their meager savings. It was difficult for non government entities such as the Salvation Army, Red Cross or even churches whose cash availabilities come from donations to provide aid. When donations disappeared, the abilities of these and other charitable organizations dried up. To help prevent individuals from failing to save for their retirement, government started the Federal Insurance Contributions Act. FICA is basically a forced savings plan for retirement. It was designed to give supplemental help to elderly folks so they could survive in retirement if hard times came about. It was never meant to be the total source of income. This fact may have been lost somewhere along the way as I believe that many Americans feel that Social Security, as FICA is now known, is their retirement. **Then WWII comes along and with its massive undertaking that firmly imprints national control and realistically, worldwide control**.

States' Rights and other non federalists did have some moments. The general feeling of getting out and staying out of Europe's mess at the end of WWI and the American Senate failing to approve the resulting Peace Treaty of Versailles were huge. As was stated before, President Wilson went around the country trying in vain to encourage public opinion to persuade the Senate. People were just glad that the war was over. They didn't want to be involved with the old world and its', continual squabbles. They were not looking ahead; they were simply ready to move on. Some of this was born out of the Progressive era. This became more than just a conservative movement as anti-war sentiment spread. During the late 20's and early 30's we had our own problems and this sentiment grew as isolationists such as Henry Ford and Charles Lindbergh became more influential. Ford during the twenties was very anti-Semitic believing that the Jews were trying to take over the world through financing and banking. Years later he apologized to the Jews.[45]Lindbergh questioned weather our planes could match the Luftwaffe or any other of the German war machines. **Pearl Harbor ended that faction's influence.**

Chapter 24 WWII

This era was dominated by rationing at home including the suspension of the food stamp program, Executive orders, and 16 million Americans in the military. Millions more Americans found work on defense projects that built over 296,999 planes, 102,000 tanks and 88,000 ships and landing vehicles. They also developed the atomic bomb through the Manhattan Project.[46] There was the draft, price controls through the office of Price Administrator, War Production Board that told you what to make, and then there was rationing. In order to control access to limited products that were being used in the war effort, **the government rationed certain products and they told you the cost.**

Women and minorities flooded the workplace. Posters of 'Rosie the Riveter' embodied the spirit of 2.5 million American women, working in factories and defense plants. African Americans were being left behind at first but after a threatened march on Washington D.C. Roosevelt issued executive order 8802 in June of 1941 stating that there would be no discrimination in the defense industries. The Fair Employment Practices Commission was established to carry out this directive. **Nothing like that had been done since reconstruction.**

But like the end of Reconstruction, amendments, new laws, or Executive orders did not eliminate the clash of races. In Detroit on June 20, 1943, Whites and Blacks rioted against each other and 34 people were killed. Also in June of 43 over 2,500 off duty soldiers and sailors attacked Hispanic neighborhoods in Los Angeles using the excuse that Hispanics were wearing 'zoot suits.' A 'zoot suit' was an oversized knee length suit coat worn by Hispanic teenagers. The over use of material was deemed unpatriotic by some and thus the excuse was made for the raid. **Racism probably had more to do with it than style of clothes and the fact that over 400,000 Mexican Americans were serving in the military was ignored.**

A major problem faced the war plants that now had the workers; where were the workers going to stay? $150,000,000 was allotted in the Lanham Act of 1940. With the creation of the National Housing Agency over two million workers were in temporary government housing. By 1943 the cost was $1.2 billion.

The **Bracero Program** was a program that **BROUGHT** Mexican farm workers in to help harvest the crops in the Southwest. This continued until 1964 and **by then it was a practice that was fully ingrained into the agricultural system.**

To pay for the war, taxes were raised. They didn't totally cover the more than $300 billion spent. To put that into perspective, that is more than all of our expenditures from the start of Washington's first term to when Roosevelt's second term ended.[47] War Bonds were issued to cover the cost. WWII is a huge topic but for the premise of this book, **it was obviously the most Federal time in our history.**

More important than our stance on size and control of government, was the dropping of two atomic bombs on Japan. Instantly thousands were killed. Millions more suffered from radiation poisoning. Should we have ushered in the Atomic Era? As tenacious as Japanese soldiers were, it has been estimated that it would take a million U.S. casualties. **Actually more people were killed in the fire-bombing of Tokyo but that did not change the world!**

Chapter 25 The Eisenhower Years

After 5 presidential losses in a row, the Republicans finally recaptured the White House with the election of Dwight D. Eisenhower in 1952. They would have done anything to win as is evident by this campaign jingo. It says, "Eisenhower hits the spot / one full general, that's a lot. / Feeling sluggish, feeling sick? / take a dose of Ike and Dick / Phillip Morris, Lucky Strike, / Alka Seltzer, I like Ike!" Eisenhower came to epitomize the new Republican as fiscally conservative, social conservative but with an international agenda. He was chosen as the Republican candidate because he could win, not for his staunch party line beliefs. In fact people were not even sure which party that Ike belonged to. He was a moderate but with him, the Republicans could win. The party had been desperately fighting Franklin Roosevelt's government expansion especially in social areas. Truman added an additional problem with the start of the Cold War against communist expansion. The Republican Party had made some inroads against the Democrats by attacking them as being soft on communism at home and abroad. China had become communist in 1949; the USSR got the atomic bomb and **Senator Joe McCarthy led an onslaught of verbal attacks on suspected communists in our government.**

Eisenhower, as President, faced several challenges in the Cold War that meant we had to have a strong defense to stop the spread of communism. His administration looked for new ways of cutting back at the same time as projecting world power. In August of 1953, at a cost of $200,000, his CIA initiated a coup to put the Shah back in charge in Iran. He instituted what he called the "New Look" [48]as he believed that the strength of America was having a strong economy. By cutting back on defense spending, it did help the economy but it also meant relying on subterfuge and on the use of atomic weapons. In January of 1954, John Foster Dulles as Secretary of State used the terms "massive retaliation."[49]That meant the United States would use atomic weapons in battles. At a press conference in responding to a question, Eisenhower compared the dangers of communistic expansion to having a set of dominoes and if one falls…**This became known as the Domino Theory.**[50]

Eisenhower faced continuing challenges on the foreign front from ending the Korean War, coups in Iran, and Guatemala and hot spots in Vietnam, Suez Canal, Hungary, and Cuba. His administration ended with the assumption that there was a missile gap in the Soviets' favor. Sputnik, a small satellite was first placed into orbit by the Soviets. The Cold War had started a race, and it looked like the Soviets were winning the 'Space Race.' Just when it looked like some real progress was being made with the Soviets under Nikita Khrushchev, Francis Gary Powers was shot down in his U-2 spy plane over USSR. Ike knew from the U-2 flights that we had a large superiority over the Soviets in missiles and there was not a 'missile gap,' but he couldn't tell because he didn't want to admit that we were spying. With so much attention called upon the government it was hard to reduce government intrusion into everyday life. **Eisenhower was able to make some modest inroads back home**.

Using his "dynamic conservatism" ideas for domestic policy, by 1954, Eisenhower had gotten a "complete overhaul of the whole Federal tax system."[51]Many aspects of the tax reform helped business. He tried to cut farm subsidies and appropriations to the TVA. He was more successful with the latter. He waved the Federal Title to the oil resources just offshore in Texas, California and Louisiana, after the previous administrations had gotten a Supreme Court ruling on ownership for the nation and used them as a Naval Reserve. He vetoed a bill to provide Federal aid to states checking pollution caused by industry in rivers. He thought that was the responsibility of the local states. He believed that "Federal aid to Education at all levels was both undesirable and unconstitutional."[52]He stopped a plan for a Federal Dam across the Snake River and gave it to private power companies. Nuclear Power plants were privately owned and built. **Some of his appointments to independent regulatory commissions were actually anti- regulation believers.**

But for as hard as the Right tried, Eisenhower working with moderate Republicans and Democrats signed much far reaching legislation. He established the Department of Health, Education and Welfare, Small Business Administration, initiated wider coverage for social security, and was instrumental in brokering a partnership with Canada opening up the St. Lawrence-Great Lakes seaway. On September 9, 1957, he signed the first civil rights act since U.S. Grant. Some of his Supreme Court nominees, most notably, Earl Warren, led the court to overturn *Plessey v. Ferguson* in the case of *Brown v. Board of Education*. The Court ruled that separate was not equal. **This led to one of the most famous showdowns between federalism and states' rights confederation.**

The Supreme Court ruling ended legal segregation. Government was to gradually comply. The showdown happened in 1957 at a Little Rock Arkansas High school where 9 Negroes, as African Americans were called then, were set to go to school. They had been selected out of a group that could withstand the pressure that would be generated. John Chanceller of NBC was filming one little girl who came by herself and had to endure the mob taunts by herself as she was turned away from school. That made the evening news around the country. Eisenhower talked to Governor Faubus and the Governor made an agreement to go slowly but to obey the law. Faubus double crossed Eisenhower. Eisenhower, after years of being the Supreme Allied Commander and now President, was not going to take insubordination. Therefore Ike ordered the 101st airborne into the city and the Arkansas State Militia to be nationalized. How much of this was retaliation to the insubornation or moving forward based on the decision of the court? **How much of this decision was based on what the national public saw that night on the nightly news?**

One of his last presidential accomplishments was the development of the Interstate Highway System that was passed in 1956. It has proven to be a great economic and recreational success, but that is not why it was built. The interstate highway was an outgrowth of a military assignment he had just after WWI when he was ordered to be in a convoy of troops and material and go from the east coast to the west coast. In large part this was ordered due to the problems incurred in France trying to move material through the mud in WWI. Eisenhower found lots of mud on the way to San Francisco from Washington D.C. 32 years later he asked General Clay, who had been the military governor of Berlin during that crisis, for ideas on a highway system to fit our military and civilian needs. The German autobahn had already shown how rapid troop movements could take place. Out of fear of a nuclear attack, a way to get lots of people quickly out of the cities was needed. SAC air bombers, it was argued, might need to land on the road in case of war. Congress would pay 90% of the bill and that was a big enticement for the states. Even though some might have believed this fear mongering, actually, the bridge overpasses were not built high enough for tanks to be trucked under. The advisory group Eisenhower used was biased, as they all had connections in some way to the road construction industry or transportation industry. **The interstate highway system was built for the wrong reasons; but it was built and every time we travel long distances, we are glad it was!**

Chapter 26 60's: Race, Violence, War, the Great Society, and Party Transformation, all seen on camera

In 1948, the Executive Order by President Truman that returning veterans should receive equal pay for their service inspired a civil rights plank that was adopted into the Democratic platform. A voting block of southern Democrats walked out of the Convention and ran their own candidate, Strom Thurmond from South Carolina. They tried to hold sway until out of practical desperation, the Dixiecrats as they were called changed political parties and became the radical, right wing conservatives of the Republican Party. This transformation took some time, but by the time of Barry Goldwater, Republican candidate for President in 1964, won in the southern states that had voted against Republican Richard Nixon in 1960, **the solid Democratic South had now turned to the Republican Party**.

Some of the reasons for the change were the Supreme Court decision of *Brown verses the Topeka Board of Education* 1954 which decided that separate was not equal. This was a reversal of *Plessey v. Ferguson*. The resultant enforcement of the new ruling in 1957 by Eisenhower was sending the National Guard to Little Rock, Arkansas, to ensure that African American students would be allowed to go to the same high school as the other students who happened to be white. John F. Kennedy through the office of his brother Robert Kennedy, Attorney General of the United States had to use similar tactics verses the University of Mississippi 1962. The Civil Rights movement gained national attention: with the bus boycott started by Rosa Parks in Montgomery, Alabama in 1955; and through the TV-captured images of the march in Birmingham, Alabama where peaceful marchers were fire hosed and set upon with dogs in May of 1963. The Economic March on

Washington and Dr. Martin Luther King's "I have a Dream" speech in August of 1963 continued the momentum. The 16th Street Baptist Church bombing in September, killing four young girls forever turned the tide. With the resulting Civil Rights Legislation of 1964, the solid Democratic South had become firmly Republican. Strife didn't end with the reelection of LBJ. The march from Selma to the Capital in Montgomery started March 7th 1965 and is known as "Bloody Sunday". **Television broadcasts showed the whole country what was really going on.**

As the Vietnam War showed every night at the supper table, the 60's were a violent time for all of us. Race riots, assassinations, peace demonstrations, and the drug culture all added to the political turmoil. Add in the continuing migration of African American to the industrial northern cities such as Cleveland, Detroit, Philadelphia and Chicago. The attitudes and the demographics of America were changing as millions of African Americans left the south and millions of snow birds (white retirees) went south. **Retirees tend to be conservative and the majority of northern migrants joined labor unions who routinely vote Democratic.**

The states' rights advocates continued to be hit with setbacks. The 24th Amendment to the U.S. Constitution made the Poll Tax illegal. The 1964 Civil Rights Act gave the federal government the right to enforce desegregation. The 1965 Voting Rights Act ended many of the tools used to disenfranchise African American voters such as Grandfather clauses, and literacy tests. **A statement of defiance was made in 1968 however with George Wallace, Governor of Alabama, running for President on the American Independent Party.**

The Civil Rights Act caused problems according to Schweikart and Allen in their book, *A Patriots History of the United States*. By law the Act "ended the last legal remnants of slavery and reconstruction." But as they point out, with the proposed legislation by Lyndon Johnson, "would reenslave many poor and minorities into a web of government dependency."[53] The biggest change was in the program from the New Deal called Aid to Family's with Dependent Children (AFDC). By trying to help families without an adult male in them, the law in effect encouraged (by granting of more money) families not to stay together or even get married at all. Within 12 years, single female families increased 200%. Most of the increase was in the African American communities.

These fatherless families, stagnated in poverty, left the young boys ripe for crime and gang involvement.

During the Nixon Administration, he tried to reign in the Great Society. Some people have called Nixon's program "New Federalism." New Federalism was the practice of giving states block grants, or money without strings attached. He increased Social Security, Medicare, and Medicaid, and the availability of food stamps while trying to eliminate the Job Corps. He vetoed increases in Housing and Urban Development and tried to stop other programs by impounding the funds authorized by Congress.[54] **This was ruled unconstitutional and helped add credibility to his nick name of "Tricky Dick."**

Chapter 27 The Reagan Revolution

"I realized that the problem wasn't big business, it was big government!" Ronald Reagan said in 1960 when talking about why he switched political parties.[55] Reagan, being used to the spot light and quick with humorous one liners, brought style and polish to the White House. Even though he relied on cue cards, he had the ability to see the big picture and to simplify it for the American People. He delegated many details to his staff. He made a concerted effort to make Americans feel good again and to feel good about their country. **That confidence, he rightly thought, would carry over into the economy.**

Ronald Reagan's election brought a new symbol of success to believers in limited government. Reagan, a famous actor and Governor of California, ran on the ideas of tax cuts, inflation reduction, and national debt reduction and increased spending on national defense. He was successful on three of the four. Using a plan that his primary opponent, later Vice President and successor George Bush Sr. called **"voodoo economics,"** it became known as **Reaganomics.** It was basic supply side economics with high interest rates.[56] **It has been viewed by some to be the answer, and by others, still the answer today.**

Reagan was helped by the politicalization of the televangelist. Preachers like Jerry Falwell and Pat Robertson pushed Conservative ideas in a movement they called the Moral Majority. They pushed efforts to get back to living by the precepts found in the Bible. **In listening to their programs one can also learn about taxes and National Defense.**

Conservatives became very good at getting simple messages out to the public. Liberalism became a bad or dirty word. God was on the Conservative side. Democrats were the party of taxes and spending. **Conservatives from the South joined Conservatives from the West**

and help win three presidential terms in a row and five of the last seven before Obama was elected.

Reagan tried to reduce government spending by cuts in welfare, housing, job training, drug enforcement, mass transit and other Great Society programs left over from Lyndon Johnson.[57]

In Kenneth Davis' book, *Don't Know Much about History*, he gives evidence that Reagan's ideas were not new and that they needed a big boost to work. Reaganites pointed out that John Kennedy used a similar strategy with tax cuts in 1963. Democrat Jimmy Carter had actually proposed similar tactics and so had Republican Herbert Hoover. Hoover's plan during the Great Depression didn't work. Supply side economics was called "trickle down economics" then. Reagan's solutions put us into a recession, especially with high interest rates to combat inflation. Oil prices had helped cause the high inflation as a group called OPEC set high prices. Oil producing and exporting countries (OPEC) started to lose control by new oil developments in Mexico and the North Sea. When these new groups undercut OPEC, the economy started to boom! The wealthy really benefited from this boom but at the same time Reagan's government spending cuts were primarily aimed at the poor. There was another problem. The nation's debt continued to rise; this was caused by the increased spending on defense. **The cuts in spending did not match the increase.**[58]

Schweikart and Allen in their book, *A Patriots History of the United States*, deny that it was the fault of defense spending.[59] They admit to a slight increase in defense spending but conclude that more of an increase was attributed to the Democratic Congress spending on social issues. They attribute some of Reagan's success to his personality. Known as the Master Communicator, he was supported by some luck. On his inauguration, the hostages being held by Iran were released. Reagan did not have anything to do with the hostages. This was a publicity stunt by the new radical Islamic State of Iran. President Carter's administration had been stalled by the apparent swelling of American impotency in solving the hostage crisis. Reagan became the immediate benefactor of the hostage's release. Reagan earned lots of respect for his recovery from a dastardly assassination attempt that brought about sympathy but also a well deserved appearance of real life personal toughness. Business saw a surge in patents and that included the explosion of computer technologies. Thousands of new jobs were created. These new jobs contrasted to the old jobs lost in heavy manufacturing like steel. Those areas became known as the 'rust belt' and were depressed, but the boom was on in Silicon Valley. Many people like to argue that Reaganomics was the answer. Others say it was the cause of the widening gulf between rich and poor and the withering away of the middle class. **Regardless of the continuing argument on Reaganomics, it had and still has a great effect on us.**

It is still about taxes
Since Ronald Reagan's name is invoked some much in our current discussion it is a good place to put this information about taxes. Black's Law Dictionary describes direct taxes as having four purposes.
- Revenue: Income to be used for operating expenses.
- Redistribution: Spreading of wealth around.
- Repricing: Upping the price of items we don't want you to buy such as cigarettes, alcohol, or protective tariffs on goods from other countries. One could lower the price on items also.
- Representation: In exchange for the right to tax us we have the right hold the government accountable for better governance.

Reagan and the Republicans like to think of revenue. They believe that with lower taxes, more business volume is created and more money is collected as Revenue. Also by cutting back on spending, less is needed to be spent.

Democrats feel that tax cuts should be made for the middle Class as that is really the driving force. To help do that a redistribution of wealth is needed. To justify higher tax rates look at this example of two persons each having a business. One business is a Mom and Pop store and the other is a multinational conglomerate. Both catch on fire. Who needs the better fire station? What is that worth? **Who has the most to lose? Who should pay more?**

During the first 75 years of our existing, protecting tariffs were our major source of income. American manufacturing was protected from overseas manufacturers especially Great Britain. The South was taken advantage of however by New England over these tariffs. Today, by lowering the price of Ethanol Gasoline in Iowa and elsewhere to make sure that you use more of it is an example of changing the price for more consumption. **Most of our examples are of raising the price if we want to discouraged usage like the added tax on cigarettes.**

Taxes can be complicated as the gas tax is a great example. Not only is the tax on gas usage sometimes reduced in order to encourage the development of new technologies. It also helps pay for the construction and repair of the roads that the gasoline users drive on.

Representation was the big catch word for the anti tax rallies in the Revolutionary day. "No taxation without <u>representation</u>." It is gaining force again with numerous people, some of which like to be called Tea Party members. They don't hold a monopoly on holding the government accountable for better governance but they think so. **This was the face of the 2010 mid term election.**

Chapter 28   Federal Excess

Four egregious examples of Federal abuses (and there are many more) are going to be discussed here. All have occurred during war times and one hopes that they were done out of real concern for our country or that would be the most egregious and outrageous. **There might not have been a great alternative to these abuses of power.**

1. Two months after the Japanese bombed us at Pearl Harbor on December 7, 1941, using Secretary of War's advice, President Franklin Roosevelt, issued Executive Order 9066.[60] Over 120,000 Japanese-American's most of whom were native born citizens were rounded up and placed in relocation centers. Most were given very little time to get family items or conclude their business. This was done at the same time that the Jews were being rounded up in Europe for a more perverse but still racist purpose by the Nazi. The American policy had a few flaws such as only Japanese Americans living in Arizona, California, Oregon, and Washington State were removed. Japanese Americans on the Islands of Hawaii **were not removed. Thousands of second generation Japanese, known as Nisei, fought in Europe and were one of our most 'heroic combat units ever.'**

What would cause a President to issue such an order? First of all, we had been negotiating with Japan just as the surprise attack on Pearl Harbor happened. This 'sneak attack,' while an act of war, also went against our sense of fair play. There had already been a prejudicial movement against the Japanese on the West Coast, trying to stop their immigration to there. Because of their distinctive racial look, it was easy to discriminate against them. Germans and Italians, whom we were also at war with, did not receive this kind of treatment. The West Coast was in a frenzied watch, expecting an attack. This paranoia could have been more exploited had news of the single or double man mini subs on the West Coast or the balloon bombs in the Oregon mountains worked. Even with news black out, there were rumors. In order to prevent hysteria and physical retaliation against the Japanese Americans, Roosevelt thought that removal was the best option. It was racist, simply racist, as shown by the words of the U.S. Army Commander in charge when he said, **"The Japanese race is an enemy race..."**

The Supreme Court ruled in *Korematsu v. United States* in 1944, that the Japanese Americans weren't removed because of their race but because of 'military urgency.' The government was also told that American citizens could not be held against their will for long. In late 1945, the Japanese were released from their Relocation Centers. Many could not go back to their former homes or businesses as they had been lost. Many more did not want to go back; they wanted to start new. In 1948, the Evacuation Claims Act released more than $31 million dollars for lost property. **The reimbursements came to less than $.10 on the dollar.**

In 1988, Ronald Reagan apologized and the United States Congress, in a weak attempt at saying we were wrong, voted a payment of $20,000 to any survivors of the Relocation Centers. What they and the nation had lost was worth way more than that. **Dignity doesn't have a price**.

One of the unique ironies of this was that on April 29, 1945, members of the famed 442 Rainbow Division, 552nd Field Artillery Battalion made up exclusively of Nisei soldiers helped to liberate parts of the infamous Dachau Concentration Camps complex. Meanwhile their parents, siblings, and grandparents were back in the United States in our internment camps. **(Note: the camps were called relocation centers, internment camps and on one occasion concentration camps by FDR.)**

2. In August of 1964, President Lyndon Johnson reported that a ship, the U.S.S. Maddox, in international waters was attacked by torpedo boats of North Vietnam. Two days later it was attacked again. This escalated and President Johnson asked and received permission to retaliate against North Vietnam. Congress overwhelmingly voted to allow the President to "take all necessary measures to repel any armed attack against the forces of the United States and to prevent further aggression." [61]**With only two opposing votes in Congress, this Gulf of Tonkin Resolution began the biggest escalation of what is now known as the Vietnam War.**

We now know that the first attack was during action by South Vietnamese boats attacking in North Vietnam and the U.S.S. Maddox was supporting them with tactical information. The second attacks never happened. Even at the time, there was evidence that weather had caused some mechanical misrepresentation on the sonar scopes and had sent some false readings. This then was the excuse to do what the President wanted to do. This wasn't the first time a President had positioned troops to cause an incident that would incite an armed attack on us that would in turn justify our overwhelming response. In 1846 President Polk, who wanted to expand America to include California, ordered General Zachary Taylor to cross the Nueces River in Texas. We were in negotiations with Mexico but they were not progressing. The Nueces River was a disputed boundary with Mexico. Texas said that the boundary was the Rio Grande. **Mexico of course attacked us and we then claimed that we were on American soil and thus went to war with Mexico and won New Mexico and California just as Polk had wanted.**

In Vietnam, it would not turn out the way we wanted it to. Some people thought that South Vietnam could turn into a California type economy but that was not our main interest in Vietnam. Our foreign policy from Truman, through Eisenhower and Kennedy had been one of strong resistance to Communism. In 1954 when the French were driven out of Vietnam, two countries were created. Although Communism was a big concern to the modern world, to most Vietnamese it was not. Many Vietnamese viewed the arrival of America as just another colonial master and a way to get rich. We played nation maker and king maker as South Vietnam was rocked with coups. **In the end, America became a divided country over the war and more than 55,000 Americans lost their lives as America lost sight of our ideals.**

3. Unfortunately, in time of war we seem to let our values slide in view of perceived National Security. In September of 2001, a small group of radical Islamic Terrorists accomplished an unbelievable simultaneous raid on very real symbols of American strength. Using transcontinental jet airliners full of fuel as weapons, terrorists crashed planes into the Pentagon in Washington D.C. and two into the Twin Towers of the World Trade Center in New York City. **The Trade Center had been attacked years earlier with car bombs being placed in the basement parking.**

Fortunately some very brave Americans forced the crash of a fourth plane, (United flight 93) into a field in Pennsylvania. These brave people accomplished two major things. First, the most obvious of all was preventing that plane from being a weapon attacking the Capital Building, White House or maybe even a populated area. The other major accomplishment was to end the use of hijacked passenger planes as weapons. The first plane passengers didn't believe or even imagine that they were being used as a bomb. The last plane knew that they would, just as all Americans now know that we could be. Once certain of their fate, these brave people made sure that the terrorists' plan would be thwarted. **The first response in the war on terrorism proved that Americans would sacrifice their lives in defense of our country.**

After all, the last line of the Star Spangled Banner does say "home of the brave" but the first part says "Land of the free". That is why the passing and application of the Patriot Act calls for a watchful eye by all of us to maintain our freedoms. Was it really necessary or was it reactionary? **It was passed in an atmosphere that our Founding Fathers so intelligently foresaw to allow for immediate action tempered with checks and balances so that actions are not purely emotional reactions.**

In this atmosphere, America allows itself to be sidetracked. Ted Koppel, a famous newscaster of Night Line fame wrote a piece about our response of 9/11. It appeared on the 9th anniversary of those attacks. He agrees that our initial response was just about right. We rapidly broke the Taliban's power in Afghanistan and chased Al-Qaeda into Pakistan. We should have finished the job. Our sidetrack is an example of federal excess. President Bush changed gears and didn't finish the job of eliminating all of the apparatus that led to Al-Qaeda's ability to attack us. Instead the Bush Administration used the emotion of the time to remake American Policy into one of pre-emptive attacks on suspected terrorist positions. This has had a two bladed effect. Some of the targets were legitimate and some were not. Sometimes there was collateral damage. We know what our feelings would be if another government was doing that here. But the biggest preemption was making the case of the connection of Al-Qaeda and Iraq. **This transfer of the emotion from the 9/11 tragedy put us into two simultaneous wars.**

One of the stated reasons for the 9/11 attacks on the United States stems from the Gulf War when American troops used part of a Saudi

Arabian dessert as a staging area. Even though we had permission from Saudi Arabia evidently we did not get Bin Laden's. Now just a few short years after the successful Gulf War conclusion, not only was Saddam Hussein involved, we were now persuaded that he had weapons of mass destruction and the means to deliver them. With our new policy of preemptive strikes, the Bush administration masterfully maneuvered Congress and the American people to believe it to be true. **We went to war with Iraq and destroyed Saddam Hussein.**

We did something else; we caused the connection of Al-Qaeda and Iraq. Now Islamic radicals did not have to travel to the United States to fight against the "Great Satan" as we are sometimes referred to. Our President even encouraged them with his infamous "Bring it on" statement. **Egyptian President Hosni Mubarak said "Before you invade Iraq there is one Osama bin Laden, after you invade there will be hundreds".**[62] He was right.

Where was our Congress in all of this? They too believed in the weapons of mass destruction. Maybe this belief was in some ways a guilt feeling since we have had thousands of such weapons and now the thought that they could be turned on us was indeed frightening. As time went on and casualties went up and no weapons of mass destruction were found, many Americans began to doubt our purpose. The underground comments about President Bush just wanting to finish what his Father didn't, and since Bush had been an oil man we were just in it for the oil, started to be loudly heard. Who knows the real reasons why we got into Iraq, but a clue comes from Dick Chaney. According to Richard Clarke in his book *Against All Enemies,* Chaney and Bush believe that weapons of mass destruction might still be found and **if you just keep saying it, most Americans will believe it.**

In the very beginning of this book I stated what I felt to be of upmost importance that we make decisions based on facts and not on repeated lies.

According to Clarke, most Americans believe that President Bush didn't do much about terrorism before 9/11 even though there were some warnings. There was no Iraq connection to 9/11. The Bush administration began planning to invade Iraq before 9/11. There was no Iraq- Al-Qaeda connection. There were no weapons of mass destruction and that information saying that there was came from Iraqi exiles who wanted a change of government in Iraq. They were paid millions of dollars by us to tell us what we wanted to hear. We really had no good plan for administering Iraq after the attacks and we didn't have enough troops to adequately and properly administer Iraq. If Clarke is right about those assumptions, how did we allow that to happen? **It is obvious that the pendulum had swung very far to the Federalist side with big government clearly in control.**

Of all of the things that Clarke says, I really believe that he is correct in this. **Our conflict is not a clash of Civilizations.** It is not the modern version of the Crusades nor should we make it so. Islam has some divisions in it just as Christianity does. Christians were not always civil to each other either. **We need Muslims to help solve the problems. That is why recent Muslim-- based controversy here in the United States is very counter productive.**

4. The last of the Federal excesses happened not in war time but in a time of great stress. At the end of the Bush administration, the economy was failing. Because of problems on Wall Street, some caused by people buying homes way out of their market range, financial business started to fail. Some were very large. As some failed, it came to a point that the Administration felt that if some of the bigger institutions failed, our country and the world would be thrown into a deep and dangerous depression. 'Too big to fail' meant that for National Security as well as economic stability we had to prop up these businesses. **Billions of dollars went into this rescue and at the same time, it came out on credit, enlarging our national debt.**

The new Obama Administration continued to rescue large auto makers trying to save jobs. They enacted a stimulus package, all trying to stem the tide of business cutbacks resulting in very high unemployment. It looks now as if the tide has turned and things are not getting worse, but they are moving at a snail's pace for recovery. Of course many people think that this is a big socialistic shift and that it was planned all along. It is simply federalism working at its best to try and do what they think is in the best interest of the country at this time. **Since both Republican and Democratic Administrations shared this federal response, is it any wonder that a movement (Tea Party) going back to confederation beliefs picked up steam?**

Chapter 29   A Curious Rise of the South

Curious is the proper word as I see that most of our discussion has dealt with problems in the South. The South has had an inherent problem that still exists in 2010. The ACT test scores show that 9 of 11 former Confederate States are under the National Average while only 3 of the 21 former Union States are under. Using any other configuration no other area comes close except when adding the Southwest. In the past 16 years two Northern states of Michigan and Illinois have slipped joining West Virginia as being under the national average where as North Carolina has improved to join Virginia as being above the national average. **This would be an interesting study to determine the reasons why this situation exists. Regardless, we know that Education is the key to Success.**

The South is making good use of some of its natural resources; agriculture has branched out from cotton and tobacco to include all kinds of fruits and vegetables besides Florida Orange Juice and Georgia Peaches. Seafood from the Gulf of Mexico is served throughout the country. Lumber is a lucrative product. Industry, especially Oil refineries have grown. NASA has been huge in Houston, Texas, Huntsville, Alabama, and Cape Canaveral Florida (also called Cape Kennedy). The warm weather has enticed thousands of 'snow birds' to migrate to the South during the winter. **Tourism is big business.**

Corporate America has found the South. Of the top four cities having the most Fortune 500 headquarter, three are in the South. Following New York City with 42, Houston has 24, Dallas 12 and Atlanta 10. Atlanta has been reborn and is the headquarters for Coca Cola and Delta Airways, Home Depot, UPS and AFLAC just to name a few. Their recovery has been so successful they held the 1996 Summer Olympics there! Lots of new and exciting innovations are coming out of the South. Just a few years ago a **curious part of the Rise of the South was coming from four surprising avenues of interest.**

First is the Country Western Music phenomenon, grown out of the Appalachian Mountains where Scottish, Irish and Scotch-Irish immigrants played and sang how they felt. In the 1920's with the advent of recordings and then WWII, a combination of sound from the West and the South was formed. Traditionally all-white performers sing about love, divorce, crime, prison, and patriotism. The traditional center piece is the 'Grand Ole Opry,' located in Nashville Tennessee and has broadcasted a weekly show since 1925. **It has a growing market.**

Second is the advent of the College Football Bowl Games. Some great Southern salesman must have said to the Northern teams: after your season is over, and there is snow on the ground so that you can't practice, why don't you and your team and your fans come on down and spend millions of dollars here to help us out; oh yeah, our Southern teams will be able to practice all the time because of nice weather. Well either through arrogance, pride or just a desire to get out of the cold, universities agreed to come down and sometimes they got upset. Surprised? Not really, with lack of practice and change of climate by only one team, the playing field has not been level. Northern schools are losing their excuses for losing now as just about every university has an indoor practice facility where they can control the climate. **As for spending the money, that has now become a tradition.**

Third is related to the second in that it involves college students. I am talking about the ritual which is known as 'Spring Break.' Southern resort cities have enticed rich Northern college kids to take their Spring Break in the warm and wet waters of the South. It has become a multibillion dollar business. Marti Gras in New Orleans is not quite at the same time and it was started for religious reasons. Also, even though they want tourists to come, **I think that New Orleans would celebrate regardless.**

The fourth and final tribute to the rise of Southern culture is NASCAR. NASCAR stands for the National Association for Stock Car Auto Racing. It grew out of a combination of speed and prohibition. Daytona Beach was the site of several land-speed records between 1927 and 1935. Some people that made illegal liquor during prohibition would deliver their product in cars that were modified to outrun police cars. After the end of Prohibition, many people still liked moonshine.

Moonshine liquor is produced without paying taxes on the product. So the fast cars designed to elude police during prohibition were improved and continued to be used to escape the tax man. In 1947 Bill France Sr. began to organize NASCAR. Within recent memory, NASCAR has made a dramatic jump in popularity in sporting events, being surpassed only by Pro Football. **They are currently tying in NASCAR advertisements on Pro football games**.

Chapter 30   2010

In 2010, the Confederation view has not remained totally static. Like all things alive it has had to evolve and change. For the most part, a reluctant acceptance of the Federal Government has happened. I have to say "for the most part," because of the statement by Texas Republican Governor, Perry about the possibility of Texas seceding from the US. This statement was made for political purposes in early 2010 to get right wing Republican support so he would maintain their support in the upcoming primary race where he was facing a stiff conservative opposition, but it was still made. Perry not only won the primary but also rode the landslide to be re-elected as Governor of Texas. (A personal note here: I believe that the Civil War answered the question of succession and to use it for any reason is vile and crass even treasonous. It disrespects all of the combatants on both sides of that war.) But with that exception, there has been a determined effort and desire to change, or water down, and perhaps even partially control the political scene. **Several states have passed a non binding resolution reaffirming the sovereignty of their state.**

The Republican Party of 1864 ran the Civil War; they fought the war in the South, passed the reconstruction laws and basically had their way with the South. The Republican Party of 2010 believes in limiting the Federal Government, cutting spending, lowering taxes, being conservative and having a strict interpretation of the Constitution. **That is a change of 180 degrees on almost any scale.**

The basic tenants of the conservative view are to keep the Federal Government small, lower taxes, replace incumbents, cut the deficit, and maintain a strong national defense. Is that born out of the Civil War experience? National defense relies heavily on a big government system. It seems like a conflict of interests. Ronald Reagan became a two term president with these views. Reagan did place a major emphasis on national defense. To pay for that, he had to borrow. Our national debt went from 32.5% of GDP to 53.1%. His trickle down economic policy didn't generate enough taxes to cover the cost of defensive increases in spending. People had jobs and the feelings in the country were predominantly optimistic. It can be argued that with Reagan's Star Wars ideas and the fact that every American kid has become addicted to video games that use the same joy stick as the F 16 fighter jets; in order to try and compete with that, the Soviet Union submerged into a sea of debt that they, the Soviets, could not rise from. This was not the only pressure placed on the Soviet Union but it did play a major role in the breakup of Soviet Union. **They may have simply gone broke before us.**

George H. Bush continued Reagan's policies and the debt continued to climb 15% more. Under Bill Clinton, the debt began to fall 9.7%. George W. Bush had the biggest rise in debt compared to Gross Domestic Production, 27.1%.[63] Does that mean that the size of government matches increase of national debt? Congress usually appropriates nearly all that the President asks for, but they can change the priorities. As a concurrent resolution, the President does not sign nor can he veto the budget. **Does Congress, which has control over spending bear the responsibility for spending or does the President?**

George W. Bush's reaction to the 9/11 attacks pushed the United States into a huge swing towards a larger government. With wars in Afghanistan and Iraq, and basically on terror everywhere, Republicans adopted policies that some people could compare to the Federalist President John Adams. The Alien and Sedition Acts are comparable to the Patriot Act and policies of questionable tactics of gathering information, such as water-boarding and wiretapping of Americans. This was all done under Homeland Security. The budget deficit skyrocketed. With lack of enforced oversight, the stock market, housing market, home mortgages, and questionable loans threatened to take the deep recession into a depression. Bush's solution was large bailouts of business's that were deemed "too big to fail". Obama was forced to continue those policies and deal with new failures. With the victory by Barrack Obama, the Republicans had a period of introspection. They have reverted to basic Reaganomics. That is: cut taxes, cut government spending, maintain a strong national defense and reduce the deficit. **To new proposals,**

they just said no. Now they will have to propose, and that is always harder than a short answer.

As a former History teacher I must interject that some of us failed in teaching basic economic terms. In private and on the public airways I have heard many misuses of the terms communism, fascism and socialism. So in case you were sleeping that day, these terms talk about ownership and control. Fascism is individual ownership with government control. Socialism is government ownership of certain businesses. Communism is an extreme form of Socialism where the state owns and controls all of the businesses. There are many variations of this. The Soviet Union style called Marxist/Leninist added religion as a tool by the rich to keep workers down and destitute. The Soviet Union had no bigger hatred than against the fascist government of Germany led by Adolf Hitler and the other Nazis and vice versa. An example of fascism is when Hitler told Alfried Krupp to manufacture ammunition for WWII and he did, Krupp as an individual owner, made the profits. We in the United States have a mixed economy with predominantly individual ownership and control. The exceptions have to do with minimum wages, safety, and equal opportunity mostly. We do have a few state owned entities dealing mainly with health care. Medicare, Medicaid, FICA (Social Security) U.S. Post Office, various state and local utilities are some examples of state owned businesses in the United States. **During national emergencies we have instituted temporary price and wage controls and also production controls.**

In the modern era of media everywhere and 24 hour coverage, one would think that radicalism would be diminished. The opposite seems to be true. Fringe groups seemed to have mastered the use of the media better than the users of the media have in recognizing tainted information. The popularity of radio and cable T.V. celebs such as Glen Beck, Rush Limbaugh, Keith Olberman and Rachel Maddow show interest in fringe groups. By being more radical, small groups can call more attention to themselves. Take the Florida Pastor Terry Jones of the Koran burning debacle for a memorial of 9/11 as an example. He only has about 30 members at church on Sundays but by his radical stance, he is able to generate worldwide interest including inciting passions to rise without money, power or a constituency. **He has singlehandedly turned the remembrance around the world, of the terrible attack on the U.S. into America attacking the Moslem world.**

Building the proposed Mosque in New York City near ground zero has also had a similar effect. The group that has not even raised any money to start this project has stirred up emotions. People are so angry at the inference of an Islamic religious building, looking like a symbol of jihad success, by building so close to Ground Zero. In reality, the site is a couple of blocks away and is currently being used by a betting shop and a 'gentlemen's club'. The Mosque is meant as a learning center and a peace promotion through understanding. **We will be exposed to more and more examples of people having exponentially more influence than their status deserves.**

The new politics will have to learn how to regulate their effect. William Randolph Hearst of the newspaper publishing world had this power 112 years ago with the coverage of the sinking of the Battleship Maine and the resultant war with Spain. Hearst and others had an agenda. He was in a competitive fight for more readers. Hearst and Joseph Pulitzer routinely sensationalized stories that had questionable veracity. The great artist Fredrick Remington had been sent to Cuba by Hearst. Remington reported that there was little chance of a war. Hearst reportedly replied, "You furnish the pictures, and I'll furnish the war!"[64] A big force in the decision to go to war was the sinking of our ship the U.S.S. Maine. Although not definitive, to us today, the sinking of the Maine looks like an accidental explosion of the forward gun powder magazine and not sabotage or the result of a mine explosion. **Regardless of the truth, Yellow Journalism and other factors in Cuba led to the Spanish American War and the battle cry, "Remember the Maine!"**

The Republicans finally have gotten tired of being the party of no and have given us a list of 5 specific ideas that they will try to enact during the next two years. They called it," The Pledge to America".

- Make permanent the Bush Tax Code.
- Cancel all unspent Stimulus funds.
- Repeal Health Care
- Include in a new health plan limitations of Malpractice suits.
- Block the moving of Guantanamo detainees from there to the United States.

Are these ideas going to be enough to satisfy both the Tea Party and Independent voters? They were enough for the election but will they be enough to govern? **This idea was based on the 1994 Contract for America that was new, refreshing, and effective.**

I thought that American military bases and our Embassies were considered by law to be American Territory, and thus equal to anywhere in the United States. I therefore don't understand the fear of detainees being placed in super maximum security prison that is actually in a state.

Comedy in Politics? To most of us, so much of what goes on in Washington is so funny that it is sad. To counter conservative Glenn Beck's "Restoring Honor" rally at the Washington Monument of August 28, 2010, Stephen Colbert and Jon Stewart have contrived to have their own rallies on October 30, 2010. Colbert's was called, "March to Keep Fear Alive", and Stewart's was called, "Rally to Restore Sanity." Beck said that he didn't realize that it was the 47th anniversary of Martin Luther King's march, but liberal comedians Stewart and Colbert knew that theirs was on Halloween. Some of this is done for entertainment purposes, and some is done to make political statements. All of this shows how much politics has become big business. Millions of dollars are being spent on trying to get a political office. Some candidates have spent multimillions of their own money. Unknown groups with patriotic sounding names are producing political ads for millions of dollars. **Who is buying our elections?**

With the emergence of the Tea Party, and a slow and small recovery from the great recession, opponents to President Obama's agenda have gained momentum. With the drain of nearly 9.6% unemployment, the polished image of hope has lost its luster. America is used to fast foods, instant coffee, ATM machines that give money immediately. **Are Americans willing to wait to see fruition of long-term corrections of the system, or are we willing to jump into the anything-but-what-we-are-doing-now mode**? Americans don't like to wait.

I am concerned about the political atmosphere that we are breathing now. I don't believe that the election will soothe our concerns. There is so much anger and misinformation out there. I read some blogs the other day that were so angry and virulent that I couldn't really tell which side they were on. It reminded me of a time when I was a senior in high school and I was coaching a 6th grade boys' basketball team in a big Midwestern tourney sponsored by the YMCA. In the championship game, played at the School for the Deaf, we were down two points in the fourth quarter. We scored to tie the game but the kids keeping score gave the points to the other team. Being a young and inexperienced coach, I confronted the scoring table by yelling and screaming about the injustice done to my team. Eventually I got two points but they didn't take the two points away from the other team and we lost the championship by two points. I learned some valuable lessons in that game as a coach. My anger, my rants and raves, you see, fell on deaf ears-- literally. I only realized later that since we were playing at the School for the Deaf, the score keepers were deaf. **My ranting and raving showed them my anger but it did not solve the problem.**

Part of my mission in writing this book is to promote political discourse. It was written to encourage political awareness and involvement, which should be done in a civil and mature way. My anger and ravings about the incorrect basketball score did not get me the desired result. I did not feel better, but I did learn. I accepted the outcome and went on to coach in over 1000 more games and had a Hall of Fame coaching career. But what will the voters learn? **I hope that the American Public will show the world again that democracy really does work; no matter how we feel about the direction the pendulum is swinging.**

Chapter 31   Tea Party

Many people, not just Republicans felt that introspection was necessary. They didn't like what the Democrats or the Republicans were doing. Reducing the deficit, although stated by the Republicans, did not happen under Reagan, George H. Bush or George W. Bush. In the last 50 years, it only happened under Bill Clinton. As more people were dissatisfied, they wanted a complete change. **As a result, the Tea Party movement of today invokes the colonial fervor of anti-establishment equating the British government of 1770's with today's federal government of the United States.**

While both exhibit some dissatisfaction with the government, they are not the same. Again, no taxation **without representation** is the biggest difference in the original tea party's beef with the Crown. The original tea party wasn't exactly as it seemed either as problems in Boston had been brewing for some time. (We know that they really weren't Mohawk Indians.)There is also evidence that many a Bostonian businessman would be hurt by the new lower price on tea as the British East India Tea Company gained the right to direct-selling of tea. This would have included John Hancock who was rumored to be one of many American tea smugglers. The Masons, meeting at the Green Dragon Tavern in Boston did however like to sing, "Rally Mohawks, bring out your axes, and tell King George, we'll pay no taxes!" [65] Our George Washington did not like the Boston Tea Party as he thought it counterproductive to stir up Great Britain when the use of boycotts had proven more effective. Nevertheless, the current Tea Party movement has gotten unprecedented media coverage. This has all been a bit puzzling as the rallies bring in speakers such as Sarah Palin. Palin is a popular figure who many consider a top contender for the Republican Presidential candidate in 2012. **I think that she will actually run as the Tea Party's first presidential candidate.** The puzzlement is in the movement. Is this a new third party or a conservative wing of the Republican Party? **Regardless of my bewilderment, they got millions of dollars of free air time and were able to get their political message out without having to pay for most of it.**

In the absence of a real set of contending spokespersons, Sarah Palin has stepped up. She has accomplished more than the first major party woman vice presidential candidate Geraldine Ferarro. She has been a catalyst for bringing the opposition together and rallying their cause. After the election of Barrack Obama, the Republicans were in sad shape and there was even talk of their demise. That is not the case today. Palin, although assuming a celebrity status, may not be able to transfer that status to being a viable candidate. On one hand she is able to draw and motivate potential conservative voters. On the other hand, she is able to generate tremendous amounts of negative feedback, supplying the liberals with equal motivation. She seems to have some qualities the Ronald Reagan had of personality, celebrity and Teflon. What is Teflon? Teflon was a brand product of a non stick coating used on fry pans. Reagan had that quality of negatives not changing the way the electoric felt about him. Palin in the midst of a conservative movement, resigns as Governor of Alaska. A truly conservative precept would be to faithfully serve her term in office as the result of the election process. **That hasn't seemed to stick to Palin as the conservatives are willing to overlook that as she is serving a larger cause.**

Sometimes people feel that they can't win in the election process so they chose to complain that the government doesn't listen to the people. That is why we vote. The vote is the poll. In this day of multi-media and instant messaging, are we becoming a body politic that demands governing by the current direction of the wind? Our founding fathers put in place a system of governing with checks and balances. Our tradition has been to accept the outcome of elections and try to make the new policies work. Founding Father John Dickinson said "whenever the public resolutions are taken, though to regard them though opposite to my opinion as sacred… and join in supporting them as earnestly as if my voice had been given for them." Thus I was dumbfounded when I heard a guy on street corner advertising for a Tea Party meeting to complain about high taxes just after Barrack Obama was elected. Obama claimed in his campaign that he would cut taxes for 98% of the American public. Before he was even in office, the Tea Party Movement began. **It did remind me of action taken before another President from Illinois took office by people who couldn't wait to see what would actually happen**.

First impressions are sometimes hard to change. The first thing I saw on the Tea Party web site was "Join and Donate." Immediately I was led to the conclusion that in this group, ideals are not the top of the list. I fully realize that in order to get anything really accomplished, money will be involved. In reading about how to promote ideals in the Freedom Works kit, comparing the original Tea Party to today, "Remember it doesn't take a majority to prevail but rather an irate, tireless minority keen to set brush fires of freedom in the minds of men.**" Money and attitude then were my first impressions of the Tea party.**

Through further investigation, I did find the "Contract from America" by Ryan Hecker, instead of Newt Gingrich and Dick Armey and the Republicans 1994 'Contract with America.' It is a good idea for a group to say what they would like to stand for. This list comes from a combination of e-mails sent to a web site. I found it very interesting that the number one concern was the constitutionality of each proposed bill and the number five concern was to audit the federal agencies for their constitutionality. These people believe that the Supreme Court and the other courts are not doing their job. That makes it a clean sweep. According to some Tea Party members, all three branches of government, the Executive, Legislative and now Judicial branches are in need of extra supervision. I find it interesting that people in government can't be trusted, but business regulations are not needed because people in business can be trusted. Other concerns deal with balancing the budget and limiting federal increase of spending to inflation and population growth; some anti-Obama administration stands on Cap and Trade; repealing health care,; use all above energy sources; reduce earmarks; and make permanent the Bush tax cuts. One did catch my eye and that was simplifying the tax code. In coaching there is an axiom called KISS. It stands for Keep It Simple Stupid. Making the tax code easy for everyone to understand makes great sense. **Lots of tax preparers would be out of a job if everyone could easily fill out their own income tax forms, however.**

By using several catch phrases like, "the American people are against...," or "70 % of the American people support the new immigration law in Arizona ..."etc...people are trying to establish a direct democracy without checks and balances. Our Constitution was made with lots of checks and balances, so thought and reason would rule and fear and emotion would not. Many of the Tea Party ideas go back to the ideas that established the Articles of Confederation, such as states' rights, small limited government with a national defense. The Tea Party has a catchy name and it is different from the right wing of the Republican Party. At least that is what I have been told. However, in looking at some of their leaders, especially Dick Armey, a former Economics Professor, former Republican Congressman, former House Majority Leader, turned drug company lobbyist, turned founder of Freedom Works, **one might see the true roots of the movement**.

The Tea Party is new and generating lots of excitement, got lots of free publicity and they brought tremendous energy to the campaign and led to the success of the election. Third Party politics in the United States has been effective in the past in two ways. They bring in new ideas and then they are either absorbed into one of the mainstream parties, or as in the case of the Republican Party and their stance on restricting the spread of slavery, they absorbed some other small parties becoming a mainstream party. Sometimes they divide the votes of the nearest party allowing the opposing party to win the election. The Bull Moose Party of Teddy Roosevelt in 1912, allowing the election of Democrat Woodrow Wilson; Ross Perot getting 19% of the vote helping Bill Clinton win in 1992; and Ralph Nader's Green Party which took just enough Democratic votes to elect George W. Bush in 2000 are just a few examples. **I believe that Tea Party members are simply a political group trying to get the pendulum swinging back towards more conservative Confederation ideals.**

Will the Tea Party survive or be absorbed into the Republican Party? Will they take over the Republicans? In what ever shape the Tea Party is in, I see a concerted effort to upgrade their candidates. It is not enough to have ideas and convictions or even to act on them. **Some of their candidates were weak and it showed, Even though their run was truly remarkable, it could have been even better. In politics, one has to be able to persuade others to also act on these ideas even when they don't want to.**

Don't expect the Democrats just to lie down and take this defeat. They have learned from both the Republicans and the Tea Party. Two years ago people were wondering about the future and if there would even be a Republican Party. **With the euphoria of the crushing defeat in the House, I'm sure that some are wondering that about the Democrats now.** Maybe the Independents will form a new group called the Spirit of 1776 or the Liberals one called the Hamiltonians. If it is genuine...

The Democrats have two advantages over the Republican situation in 2008. The Democrats, despite this humiliating loss, still control the Senate and the White House. Both sides have to govern and it is easier to criticize from the stands than it is from the playing field. The Republicans/Tea Party have tremendous momentum. Will that trend increase by the next election? **Now the onus to govern is on both parties.**

Chapter 32   ODDS and ENDS

Warning: A good way to make your friends or relatives mad is to disagree with them about welfare fraud. Take a hypothetical case of 100,000 people defrauding the government of 250 million dollars and 100 businesses defrauding the government of 900 million dollars. Remember that these are clearly hypothetical numbers. Both are wrong. One group tends to get little response, but the other group elicits vehement, almost to a hatred response. One group had more actual dollars of fraud $2,500 verses 9 million dollars for the other but they get a pass. **Try using these figures with friends and family as an experiment in social behavior.**

If my observations are correct, why does that happen? Does that come from a basic belief system that is subtly stated but is engrained in the American nature? The belief is "Hard work pays off" and if someone does not follow that maxim, then they are rocking the social mores of our basic culture. **Exposed examples of greed (Wall Street) and even tax evasion (number if companies advertising their ability to reduce you tax amounts if you haven't paid taxes in years) are more accepted.**

Some prime examples of Confederation ideals are ideas right from the Constitution of the Confederate States of America. Most notably they are term limits and line item veto. Jefferson Davis was elected for a one time, six year term as President of the CSA. **He had the line item veto power.**

The line item veto was passed in the United States in 1988. It was later ruled unconstitutional by the United States Supreme Court. The late Senator Robert Byrd, the longest serving senator in U.S. history, felt that giving the President the **line item veto made the president a "Super Legislator" and took away many constitutional checks and balances.**

Term limits grow out of two areas. One is the frustration of being unable to vote out an incumbent because of the benefits he/she gets by being in the government, such as committee appointments. The free franking privilege, visibility because of media access and the power of committee control by seniority gives incumbents an unfair advantage. With term limits however, the effectiveness of a basic lame duck is very limited. Term limits can also lead to one's planning of their future, and some unscrupulous politicians might use their votes for future job opportunities. With term limits in mind, let us look at the careers of two of the longest standing Senators, Republican Ted Stevens of Alaska and Democrat Robert Byrd of West Virginia. Together, both served nearly 100 years in the Senate and both are recently deceased. One of the common themes in their eulogies was how well they served their home state. That means that they were very good at earmarks! I feel that sticking up for one's elected state is the senator's job. It is very states' rights. Sometimes, **I believe that some people who want term limits only want them for the opposing party.** It is always good to practice what you preach!

The other consideration is of the development of the professional politicians. These people can become so isolated and out of touch that they are light years away from normal citizen living. In some cases, their only employment has been in politics. Is there another way? The ancient Greeks encouraged all citizens to hold office once. When they were finished, a vote was taken to see if they had improved the office. **If they had not, they would be ostracized from that city-state.**

The line item veto and having a bill passed without a rider attached to it might be a good method of making our laws simpler, and so would the idea of majority rule. I admit to being befuddled by the 60% vote rule in the Senate. For a bill to become a law, it has to be passed by both houses in the same form and then signed into law by the President, who can Veto it if he/she desires to. These are part of the system of checks and balances from the U.S. Constitution. All of the House of Representatives and 1/3 of the Senate are up for election every two years. That is another way of constitutional checks and balances. I know that the 60% rule was put into place to eliminate the filibuster. A filibuster is the practice of trying to stop legislation that a minority vehemently opposes. Yet the party claiming to be strict constitutionalist has trouble letting the system work. 60% to pass legislation is not ramming it down the throats of the American people. It is a redundant check on Congress. It is also a very stalemating process that will lead to stagnation. Now that the Senate is closer to 50/50 in 2010, how much legislation will get passed? Even with the Tea Partyists, Republicans, Independents and who ever else is elected that ran on an outsider image, they will have to let their ideas persuade congress. That will be very difficult. The ability to read the pendulum is becoming increasingly more clouded. **Regardless of our political beliefs, our logic, and our good intentions, that pendulum is swinging.**

Some other ideas from the confederate constitution were the addition of God. In that preamble is added "invoking the favor and guidance of Almighty God." Prayer in school and the 10 commandments by most accounts would have been allowed in Confederate schools. The schools in the Confederacy in 1861 had trouble with books however; schools looked for texts that spoke up for slavery. Such texts were hard to find. Prayer is allowed in public schools in 2010. Some people get confused about directed prayer by school authorities and individual private prayer. **Individual private prayer is still allowed in schools, but slavery is not.**

Civil discourse is very important in a democracy. We must listen to what our opponents are actually saying; likewise, they must actually listen to what you are saying. Otherwise it is an argument, shouting match, voice over voice and emotions must be maintained in order for discourse to work. Free speech does give you the right to say true things at appropriate times. It also gives the other person the right to say true things back to you. **Free speech is a two way street. Too often we want that street to be one way-our way.**

Another problem with cutting taxes and the Federal Budget is that usually money to the states gets cut, or services to the people of the states get cut; therefore the state has to compensate for the aid that the Federal Government was providing. That means that the state must either cut services or raise taxes. What are your state tax rates during the period of federal tax cuts? Is it better to say that we cut taxes on the federal level when in reality, cuts in services and state tax increases add up to more taxes with less service? **I know that I would rather pay taxes and have a job than have a tax cut and not have a job.**

The next current issue is the deficit. The question is, should we spend a little more to help the economy and to make sure the recovery is really working, or should we try to pay down the National debt? Our National debt has been with us from the beginning. Thomas Jefferson figured that the total amount of debt in prerevolutionary Virginia was over 2 million pounds. He estimated that it was between 20 and 30 times the amount of money circulating in Virginia.[66] The concern of the Democratic-Republican Party of Thomas Jefferson and James Madison was that the national debt created by the federal government would bankrupt the country. 220 some years and counting under the U.S. Constitution, the concern are still the same. The real question is paying down the interest on the debt. It is a continual drain that puts a strain on our ability to run an efficient economy. That will be a problem for a long time unless we sell off lots of Federal land like we used to do. **Republican President Dwight D. Eisenhower believed that the best prevention of national debt was to have a strong economy. That proved true recently under Democratic President Bill Clinton.**

Some people have concerns about if the debt holders demand repayment. First of all, we live in a global economy and if the debt collector ever came, the havoc that it would cause would destroy the collector's currency; their loss in value of their own money would be worse than the amount of collection. Talk about a high collection rate! China, which holds most of the debt today, is a huge trading partner with us. They want our economy to be robust so their economy continues to boom. **China doesn't want us to struggle because that also hurts their economy. That is the reality in a global economy**.

We do need to get over this hump of massive deficit spending. It adds inflationary pressures to our economy. With the change in Congress, and the pendulum swinging, I believe that the Obama Administration will hold down expenditures through 2012. Think about it though: with two wars going on and the great recession to be stopped with bailouts and stimulus; with cutting the rise in health care cost; and with less tax receipts coming in, to do it all was a daunting task. **I am always reminded of the fiscal rules that I have seen cities, schools, and even people use. It is the practice of looking hard to save a nickel in the short term but then, having to spend a dime in the long term.**

My choice of calling the conservative group believers in confederation, one might feel that much of this is irrelevant and confuses the issues with the Confederate ideals. I might see the merit of that and we could have that discussion. Ideas that have some connection with history, it seems to me, warrant a second look because they have a track record. Many ideas are being put out there and some even by the party out of power. **These ideas unfortunately are not how to get things done better or improve things, but are how to stop legislation that they feel could potentially be harmful to them or their pocketbook**.

Some states are taking action to stop implementation of the new health care reform law. In a primary election, 70% of the people voting in Missouri object to parts of the law. In the general election exit polls show that it still is a high priority by 48% of the people. Mississippi joins Florida and 19 other states in court action to declare the law unconstitutional due to violation of the commerce clause of the U.S. Constitution. Most of these complainants are Republicans and most of the states involved are states controlled by Republican voters. It is interesting to note that the most controversial plan of the new health care law was actually put into practice by Republican presidential hopeful Mitt Romney when he was Governor of Massachusetts in 2006. Virginia has also contested the validity of the new law and Virginia's court case has passed a Federal Judge, a first step to getting a Supreme Court ruling. Virginia and Arizona are also contesting immigration practices. The Arizona case is the Federal Government contesting the state law saying that it is unconstitutional. These cases and others show that the political pendulum is never standing still. **Unlike measured equal swings, our political pendulum can take short, unequal, and radical changes in speed, swings.**

As you read this, you know the election of 2010 was a dramatic reversal of 2008. It will be very interesting to see and time will tell if the voters voted for or against something. As in all elections there are choices. **Unfortunately, when people vote against something, the winning politicians think that their victory was a mandate for action when it reality, it was just a rejection of the previous politician.**

By 2012, will we know if the Tea Party is a real third party or is it just the repackaged Republican Party? Will there be a Democratic Renaissance, or infighting between Clinton and Obama?

In the middle of the Civil War when things on the war front were not going the best, the Congress of the United States voted to create one of its best pieces of legislation. The Land Grant Education Act of 1862 officially, but it was known as the Morrill Act of 1862. Actually it had almost passed in 1857. That version required military studies to be included. The new version did not. 30,000 acres of public land was given to develop the Land Grant Universities. **Most 'state' Universities are Land Grant.**

As both a coach and a spectator at many sporting events, I've noticed some confusion when two American flags are present. At a typical football game there may be one flag on a pole and an honor guard carrying one flag. Which do you face to sing the National Anthem? I believe that it is the Honor Guard. **People** should take precedence over **things**, after all the Constitution begins with the words, **"We the people…"**

Chapter 33　The Future of Federalism and Confederation

While it is always difficult to predict the future unless you write in quatrains and your name is Nostradamus, our future is bright. At a high school basketball game last winter, an ice storm temporarily knocked the power off. The reason that I say that our future s bright is because of what happened in those short moments before the back up generator came on. It was the kids. There was no panic just the reaction of awe as hundreds of cell phones lit up the gym. I said in twenty years those students will be telling their kids about that game that the lights went out and the cell phones lit up the gym and their children will say, **"What is a cell phone?"**

There are two issues here that are important. Most important is our children. They won't be perfect and neither were we but they will continue to make America great. The second and also important fact to gleam from this story is how fast our society changes. **How many of you would buy stock in a wrist watch company now compared to 5-10 years ago?**

If current trends continue, our government will be bigger. Federalism has continued to expand as our population grows. Confederation beliefs are strong and doing well and they will continue to grow. It's like having a family. With your first child you love them beyond belief and one can't imagine that you have any more love to give. Then your next child comes along and your love has dramatically expanded. **You still love the first born as much as you did but the second has opened up a whole new vista.**

In the short term, I really don't see much legislative action happening before the election of 2012. With the momentum of the pendulum swinging back towards conservative confederation, the votes won't be there for any meaningful changes. Everyone will be fiscally conservative, but passing any legislation over a presidential veto will be rare if not impossible. The Democrats don't have a super majority so their legislative agenda will be stalled. The Republicans/Tea Party has momentum but control only the House of Representatives. Here is a short list of issues; needed campaign financing will not be passed as confederation forces feel that it is to their advantage to have. They will argue why should the government know if I am financially backing a candidate or not, and the federalists will say that the wealthy, and foreign governments, or businesses **are buying our votes.**

Two conservative issues of gay marriage and repealing health care will not pass a presidential veto. Some fine tuning of the health care might pass if it is properly approached to show that it is an improvement. Gay marriage is gradually becoming more acceptable and in the future it will cease to be an issue. **The religious right won a short stay on the issue and will still opposes it but with little hope of political change on that issue**.

I hope that congress can come to a meaningful agreement on the abortion issue. Both sides have been solidly entrenched for years. One side says that for religious beliefs that it is wrong, and the other side says that actually fewer abortions happen under their watch because of safety net programs etc. The arguments are endless and not effective. They don't even line up with political beliefs. The side believing in less government control wants to enforce carrying a baby to term. The side that likes to say that they are the champions of the powerless and under representatives supports choice. **I fervently hope that people realize this and instead of saying that I am "pro choice" or "I am "pro life," that they will say "I am pro adoption!"**

Two major legislation issues that I hope can be addressed are the 78 million "baby boomers" and the problems that we cause for Social Security, and Immigration reform. Social Security affects all of us and our relatives. We don't need panic stricken speakers touting about how we can't afford it. **We need creative solutions instead.**

Immigration reform will be the top issue that could be legislated. It should be addressed in a number of areas. To start with, we must slow down the number of new illegal immigrants. This can be accomplished by cutting the accessibility of jobs here. If businesses are really hurt by fines for knowingly employing illegals and they don't hire as many, then fewer people illegally come here. I just don't think that we really want to stop workers from coming here illegally. Think of how many times that we have heard of a political figure who "didn't know that they were illegal" when talking about their nanny, house keeper or gardener! In Iowa, I hear ads in Spanish designed to recruit Spanish speaking workers to work in the meat industry. **Is it any wonder why people come here?**

Next is to secure the Southern borders. With violent drug cartel activity on the rise and much nearer to the border, it becomes more of a problem. With more violence near the border and the smuggling of people, drugs and guns in and out of our country, **this should be an area of political agreement.**

The final thought is to come to some **workable solution** to the problems of the millions of illegal's who have been here awhile and are immersed into our society by jobs, relatives, citizenship of their children and community involvement. **What is needed is a pathway to citizenship that does not encourage new illegal immigration but does not try to ship everyone out of the country.**

On the Horizon After 2012

Of most importance, we can't govern by fear. We have people who believe that the last days are upon us. They are predominantly in two groups. One group doesn't think that we will be here after 2012. They base this on a collection of things but most notable is the Mayan Long Calendar which runs out in 2012. Two other major groups don't buy the end of the world in 2012. One group is made up with the scientists that work for NASA. They liken it to the reported earlier end of the world in 2000 and the Y2K bug. They say that there will be a total solar eclipse and a peak of solar sunspot activities. The Asteroid Eros will pass relatively close to us. The other group is the Mayans themselves. They have no tradition of end of the world scenarios in their history. This is the end of their 13th calendar and the beginning of the 14th. **They are more worried about rainfall.**

The other group is a small group that wants to believe that we are close to the end days and Armageddon. They are willing to help cause action to happen in the Middle East because it fits with their belief of the end of times. Catholics and others generally believe that St. John and his Book of Revelation was actually talking about the end of the

Roman World and not our world today. They say that the numbers 666 add up to Nero and not the Devil. Nero was the infamous emperor who blamed Christians for burning Rome. Regardless of your political and religious beliefs, we can't let any radical believers force a major war with the Middle East because **they** say that it says so in the Bible or any other book.

We have several other and different conspiracy manias swirling around us. Dan Brown was able to make a fortune with his Da Vinci Code movies and books. The National Treasure movies also were a big hit. On a lesser scale, I saw a face book message trying to show evidence that the U.S. has several potential concentration camps and FEMA is behind it all. FEMA even has several coffins ready for the camps. One camp near Fairbanks Alaska could hold 500,000 people. Let us look more closely at this. FEMA helps out when there is a major disaster. They provide trailers for housing and other forms of aid if there is a tornado, hurricane, earthquake or even an infectious deadly disease attack, FEMA would respond. I wonder where they keep all of the trailers when they are not in use? If an infectious disease killed many people we would want to isolate their bodies so as to prevent a further spread of the disease. Maybe that is what the coffins are for. Fairbanks Alaska could not handle 500,000 people without major economic investment in transportation, buildings, housing, food, and heat. Using some common sense, disaster preparations aren't nearly as interesting as secret conspiracies. **Beside the obvious question of why, the next question is how could we afford to do it?**

In addition to the more pressing issues mentioned such as Social Security, Health Care, Immigration reform and Campaign financing reform we have to deal with a seemly futuraristic situation. Citizenship for clones. Wow that sounds so far out of reality. But is it? The overwhelmingly general feeling of most Americans is that human cloning is immoral and illegal. **It has been done with animals and it will be done with people by someone, sometime, if it is possible.**

A closer reality is our response to attacks by robotic drones. We are using them more and more in Pakistan and it is just a matter of time before one is used against us. We have rapidly incorporated robots in Iraq and Afghanistan. We have guns that shoot around the corner so our soldiers don't have to be exposed as a target. Robots check for bombs or will enter a building where there is a possible ambush or booby-trap. We are working on E-bombs which will disrupt energy using equipment. Lots of new technicological development is essential to us. **These new developments place fewer of our soldiers in harms way.**

Terrorism is still a problem. I believe that we must do more to win the hearts and minds of the youth in Muslim countries. I feel that we should challenge the terrorist every time a bomb goes off by saying, "It is easy to destroy, but what have you built"? Maybe that shows frustration but a psychological war is safer and less expensive than a physical war. **The demographics of some Middle Eastern countries show a high number of young people and high unemployment. Both are ingredients for trouble.**

As Iraq and hopefully Afghanistan wind down, where will the next crisis be? Will it be Yemen or Pakistan or will the fires of hatred re-ignite in Iraq? Will the Mexican violence overflow into the United States?

We must be prepared both psychologically and physically to withstand cyber warfare. Interruption of our electricity grid is a prime target. Some people feel that this is too far in the future but the future is now. In October of 2010, Iran claims that a computer worm has shut down their nuclear development program. **Of course they claim that it is an attempt by the West to slow down Iran's nuclear program and it probably was.**

A very real concern is a regional one, but one that could have national repercussions. The availability of water in California, Nevada, and Arizona, especially in major population areas is closely monitored. **An unexpected change in the water supply would be devastating.**

Other areas have had problems with natural gas mixing with peoples' tap water. So much so that they can even light the water on fire! That is real fire water and it is not a joke.

Chapter 34 The Wave

This is not the wave that is created at sporting events where you have a choice of participating in it or not, but more like the waves found in the ocean, lake or even at water parks. Immigration has been described as a wave of immigrants. There have been many waves, a few, like the 1.5 million Irish coming from the potato famine in the late 1840's through the 1860's, and many Germans coming after their revolution in 1848; were huge, tsunami type waves. These dramatically changed the country. Being mostly Catholic, these new immigrants drew resentment and even a new political party of nativists formed to oppose them. The new party was called the "Know Nothing Party"[67] because of their typical answer when asked the question about their beliefs. Its official name was the American Party. In 1856, former President Millard Fillmore got 23% of the national vote. **By 1860 they had been absorbed by the Republicans.**

In the 1870's the Prussian Chancellor, Otto Von Bismarck was using war to unite many Germanic areas into a country called Germany. With lots of available land here, another wave of Germans came to the Midwest. After WWI, many Eastern Europeans migrated to the United States. America blocked a Japanese wave of immigration in 1906-08 to California. The Japanese then tried to immigrate to China and we protested that also. Some historians say this was **one of the causes for the attack on Pearl Harbor.**

Now there is a great migration or a new set of waves hitting the American shores. Right away one thinks of the Hispanic migration both legal and illegal. But concurrently, there are waves from the Middle East, Pakistan and India, and the Orient. **Combined, one could call it the "Browning" of America.**

Like the experience that you have had at the lake, ocean, or a water park, each wave moves you. After the wave hits you there is a force pulling you back and then before you get all the way back, another wave hits you. Our country is changing, but it has been constantly changing, we just haven't been able to see it so clearly. Unfortunately, some people don't want to see the changes. Their thinking is of a time when they were growing up. That time doesn't exist and will never exist again. Times are changing faster than ever, but some problems with immigrants stay the same. There has always been some animosity toward new groups. In 1798, President John Adams, a Federalist, wanted to go so far as to change the number of years that an immigrant had to be here before being eligible to become a citizen, from 5 to 14 years, because most of the new citizens were voting as Democratic Republicans and not Federalists. Later the Know Nothings wanted the eligibility wait to be 25 years. The "Irish need not apply" signs in storefronts and the anti-black sentiments of some Northern factory workers just after the Civil War are just two examples of prejudice. **Anyone who has concerns about their own employment status has an immigration issue.**

Religion also plays a big factor especially if it is in the minority of mainstream Americans. The Irish Catholics had this problem and so did the Jews, but now it is the followers of Islam. 9/11 and the resulting wars in Iraq and Afghanistan and the war on terror have fueled this concern. Some radical Muslims believe in trying to make the whole world Muslim; some who are overseas practice intolerance towards other faiths and have stringent restrictions on women compared to our modern western standards. Millions of Muslims however have been Americanized and practice their faith in peace and harmony as Americans. People forget that we are fighting <u>for</u> Muslims in Iraq and Afghanistan not just against Muslim terrorists. **Some Americans blame all Muslims for the attacks. This is demonstrated with controversies of the threatened Koran burning and Mosque building in New York near the Trade Center site.**

Do the political parties of today view immigrants as potential voters? Of course they do, but there is also the group that resists immigrants and they have their political views. Much of the rhetoric on immigration stems from this very point. Taking emotion out of the equation however, immigration groups have all greatly added to our country and especially our economy. They have also brought some of their traditions along and these have changed us. **The German immigrants brought the saying**

"knock on wood" as a form of good luck but much more influential was the Christmas tree.

Christmas in the colonies is unrecognizable to us today. Santa Claus, as we know him, is a combination of immigrant traditions that has been Americanized. In 1862, a 22-year-old Thomas Nast, an immigrant from Germany, introduced us to our modern day appearance of Santa Claus. Through Nast's cartoons, Santa now has elves and a workshop, gets letters, lives at the North Pole, only gives good children gifts, and they get them on December 25. Nast also depicted the Democrats with a donkey and Republicans with an elephant as their party's symbol. **Nast not only changed America, he changed the world.**

Thomas Paine: the Englishman who made America. Thomas Paine came to the American Colonies just in time. His Pamphlet called *Common Sense* changed the way we thought about breaking away from Great Britain. His series of writings called *The Crisis* came at an emotionally down time in the Revolutionary War. General Washington ordered the December 23, 1776, essay to be read to the troops to inspire them. Here are the first couple of lines that were read. "These are the times that try men's souls, the summer soldiers and the sunshine patriots will in this crisis shrink from the service of their country; but he that stands by it now deserves the love and thanks of man and woman. Tyranny like hell is not easily conquered"… Paine had a very big impact on us at that particular time. His life before and after was in shambles but he was a very bright star for the American Revolution. **He was the first to use the term, "The United States of America."** He also advocated both Union and Manifest Destiny with this portion of Common Sense.

"The sun never shined on a cause of greater worth. Tis not the affair of a city, a county, a province, or a kingdom; but of a continent—of at least one-eighth part of the habitable globe. Tis not the concern of a day, a year, or an age; posterity are virtually involved in the contest, and will be more or less affected even to the end of time by the proceedings now. Now is the seedtime of continental union, faith, and honor…"

Paine's vision of America is no less of a challenge to us now than it was to Americans then. We have to make it work for all Americans. We need to tend to cultivation of the seeds planted by our forefathers. We as a people need to **work together**, to have **faith** in our fellow citizens, our representatives and our country. We also need to **honor** the freedom of political ideas by being rational, informed, fair, open minded, and respectful to others. If we have a position of responsibility, we must **honor** that position by striving to do the best that we can. **I think that is still called "common sense!"**

Immigrants really have changed America. No more clearly can be this seen than in an e-mail I received the other day from a high school classmate who happens to be a Native American. She wrote, "**We used to have a problem with immigration, we called them 'White People!"**

Epilogue:

In keeping with the theme of this book, I have omitted some very significant parts of our history. The women's movement is an example. Woman Suffrage, for as long and hard as their movement was, doesn't tip the scales of our discussion of federalism or confederation as they entered on both sides. Neither did the actual fighting of the War of 1812. Some parts, like the WWII era were just too obvious to site the many examples of expanded federalism. Some parts I might have just missed an opportunity. Some parts, I felt, were just not relevant to the discussion. I have tried to include useful material to foster a better understanding of our current political system and possibly where we are headed. To conclude this book, **I have 5 major ideas and hopes that through contemplation and activation can help improve America. Are our actions driven by our beliefs, or do we arrange and assume beliefs to follow our actions?**

1. The America of today is one of complainers. Our government can't this or that. We should throw all the bums out etc. You have heard it also. I believe that we must become more positive and more optimistic. When we want change, we must ask, "Change to what?" In ancient times in Greek culture, leaders would seek guidance from the Oracle. In 547 B.C. King Croesus of Lydia asked if he should go to war. The answer was, "A great Empire will be destroyed!" He went to war and **his** empire was destroyed! We can't go back and change history even though some people clearly try to rewrite it for their purposes and it is difficult to know the future. We must make something of our time. John Kennedy said in his inaugural address, "Ask not what your country can do for you, but what you can do for your country!" **Today it seems that people are saying for the government to do this for me, and that for me, do it fast, but don't ask me to pay for it.**

2. I have real concerns about civility in politics. However; problems today are nowhere near the caning of Senator Sumner in 1858. Sumner had said some reprehensible things about another Senator, but being beat with a cane in a place of representation and discussion was not appropriate. (Both persons involved, however, became heroes for the politics they backed). The art of compromise and the will to get things accomplished seems to be gone. The people who claimed to want to change the way business is done in Washington will fail, unless they have the will to get things done and use the art of compromise. Radical tactics used for short term gains by alienating the other person's point of view will come back to be used against you. Speaking the truth would be of great benefit for everyone and not just "spin truth." **A spin truth is a half-truth when you are trying to persuade someone, and only the good points are presented.**

3. Is our technology of sound bites and 24 hour news channels moving faster than our representative government can respond? De Tocqueville said in his book *"Democracy in America"* "The very essence of democratic government consists in the absolute sovereignty of the majority; for there is nothing in the democratic states which is capable of resisting it." [68] **What if the new majority tries to trump the elected majority?**

Politicians routinely use current polls to back up their agenda. Poll based decisions or even legislation lose the system of checks and balances. The election of Barrack Obama and 60 Democratic Senators and a majority in the House of Representatives in 2008 had been challenged well before the election in 2010. Being cognitive of this trend, Agricultural Secretary Vilsack quickly fired and then had to apologetically try to rehire Ms.Sherrod who was shown to have said some racially discrimitory stuff in a sound bite on the air. After re-evaluation of what she really said in the entire speech, this showed that she was a wonderful government employee who went out of her way for all races! She had been totally taken out of context! **We can't be governed by sound bites.**

We have been brought up with rapidity. Rapid transit, instant coffee, fast foods, microwave cooking, cell phones for instant communications, and iPods all mark our pace of life. The stock market price listings, earnings, and profits must show improvement in the quarterly returns. Long term investment in either companies or people is rare. I fear that we have gotten used to rapid gratification of our needs without demanding high quality neither of return nor of personal investment in ourselves. **I call that <u>instanity</u>. It is a made up word combining instant and insanity.**

Our history is loaded with instanity. Our overthrow of the leadership in Iran in 1953 and establishing the Shah in the short-term led to Middle East stability, a buffer to the Soviets and record profits for American oil companies. **However, the long-term effects are now a radical Islamic State that threatens a major war in the Middle East with Israel.**

Another case of instanity is after helping the Mujahedeen in Afghanistan defeat the Soviet Union, we abandoned them. Now years later, some of the same leaders are fighting us in Afghanistan again. A must reading or viewing is a report by Lawrence Wright who interviewed several al-Qaeda and other Muslims and their leaders. **His view and Ted Koppel's are very similar and they warn that we are reacting just the way our enemies want.**

Bringing the issue closer to home with today's discussion of stopping deficit spending while engaged in a fragile economy; what could be the effects short and long term? What about the future of Social Security? What about the track record of the out of power party being obstructionist and becoming the majority? What lessons will then have been learned by the new minority? When I ask these questions many people say, "I don't know but I just want a change." "Things aren't working now so we should change." "I don't like the way things are going." Things and movements have to be well thought out. The new instanity used to be called knee jerk reaction. That is the natural response to the Doctor's hammer tap on our knee judging our reflex motion. **Policies must be well thought out and given time to work then they can be fairly judged. Were they fairly judged 2010? In the future, will we give more or less time to evaluate policies?**

De Tocqueville also said, "'The will of the nation' is one of those phrases which have been most largely abused by the wily and the despotic of every age."[69]

I have always thought that we should have two national monuments that really state what it is to be an American. What I have in mind are both already built, one is on the East Coast and one is on the West Coast. The East Coast one is the Statue of Liberty. It should stand for

Freedom. The West Coast one is the old prison at Alcatraz. It should stand for **Responsibility**.

4. The Statue of Liberty is known around the world. It is a gift from the French and as a gift it signifies what America is. America is a place for all people of all races and nations to come together and become one nation. America has been described as a true melting pot but it is more like a national stew. If you put a carrot in the stew it is still a carrot. If you put potatoes in the stew, the potatoes still are potatoes but the stew tastes better. I think that the water in the stew is the English language. By everyone having that common base, it touches all of the ingredients. Without the water, the different tastes do not come out to add to the stew. The freedom we have can simply be demonstrated by rotating our arms back and forth in any manner we choose. However; if someone was in that space, our right or freedom to twirl our arms is not greater than that person's right is to not get hit. **Simply stated, my rights are equal to your rights but not superior to yours.**

5. The old prison on Alcatraz Island in San Francisco Bay should stand as responsibility. We all have the responsibility to be a good citizen. By that I mean, live the Preamble of the Constitution. Instead of the Constitution being some paper in Washington D.C. let's bring it alive. Think of what America would be like if we tried to form a more perfect union by considering the needs of all of our citizens. What if we all treated each other with justice that was fair and did our civic duties by trying to obey our laws, or if we all tried to get along by insuring peaceful actions? Just think of that America: if we all tried to do our part by serving in the armed forces or taking another job to help America such as teaching or helping the sick or injured or protecting us at home. What if we all tried to help those less fortunate than ourselves by working in a soup kitchen, donating clothes or helping people who don't understand basic finances instead of exploiting them? We must use the blessings of liberty by being an informed citizen who votes and promotes American values and not just complains. Thus we put into actions the words: *"WE THE PEOPLE OF THE UNITED STATES, IN ORDER TO FORM A MORE PERFECT UNION, ESTABLISH JUSTICE, TO INSURE DOMESTIC TRANQUILLITY, TO PROVIDE FOR THE COMMON DEFENSE, TO PROMOTE THE GENERAL WELFARE AND TO SECURE THE BLESSINGS OF LIBERTY FOR OURSELVES*

AND OUR POSTERITY DO ORDAIN AND ESTABLISH THIS CONSTITUTION OF THE UNITED STATES OF AMERICA."

If we all did that, it wouldn't matter if we have Federalism or a Confederation!

The End

Craig Parkinson
cmparkin@hickorytech.net

NOT SO FAST! Please continue on with the Questions, Answers and Awards section starting with the Presidential Rankings on the next page, (page 141) and continue on to page 155, Author's note.

Ranking of Presidents as to their beliefs and actions.

Federalism:

1. Abraham Lincoln- Union, with personal tragedy, Civil War, Emancipation, Martial Law, Total War, Use of new technology.
2. Franklin Roosevelt- New Deal legislation, court packing and of course WWII.
3. Teddy Roosevelt- Trust busting and Creation of Panama and the Canal, Federal intervention in Coal strike, rank higher if something more would have been going on.
4. Lyndon Baines Johnson- Great Society legislation, Civil Rights and Vietnam.
5. Andrew Jackson-Destroyed National Bank, Indian removal, Nullification crisis.
6. Barrack Obama- Bailouts, National Heath Care, Government Motors.
7. George W. Bush- Two wars and the Patriot Act, Corporate bailouts, No Child Left Behind cancels Bush Tax Cuts.
8. Woodrow Wilson- WWI, Federal Trade Administration, Clayton Anti-Trust Act.
9. Richard Nixon-Lots of power under the table but recorded. Trade with China. Bombing in Cambodia.
10. Harry Truman- Korea, "The Buck stops here!"
11. John Adams-Alien & Sedition Acts, XYZ affair.
12. James K. Polk- Orchestrated the Mexican War to fulfill Manifest Destiny.

Alexander Hamilton would have been number 1 had he been elected President

John F. Kennedy inspired a nation with Peace Corps, Moon challenge, New Frontier, and best quote, "Ask not what your country can do for you, ask what you can do for your country." His assassination helped Lyndon Johnson's agenda. Kennedy ranks first in inspirational. We will never know how much he could have done.

Confederation:

1. Thomas Jefferson-Didn't think that the Constitution allowed him to buy Louisiana. He cut the military and other government functions.
2. Calvin Coolidge- Silent Cal, nothing to say about him but Business is America's.
3. James Madison- In with Jefferson on Nullification.
4. Jimmy Carter-Reaction from Nixon, couldn't delegate, Iran Hostages.
5. James Monroe- didn't have to do anything as he presided over the 'Era of Good Feeling.' The famous 'Monroe's Doctrine' was actually enforced by Great Britain's navy.
6. Gerald Ford- Good at restoring goodness to the office of President.
7. Herbert Hoover- did more than you think trying to stop the Great Depression.
8. Dwight D. Eisenhower-Republicans wanted him to do more but he was fighting the Cold War.

Ronald Reagan actually ranks high on both charts, massive cuts in domestic programs but equally dramatic increases in military spending and special projects.

It is very difficult for a President leaning towards confederation to be very prolific. If he is very good, he cuts spending, he cuts taxes, he cuts the size of government, he allows business a free hand with little regulation. If all of those things are true, and he has had a good presidency, what can you write about? The word cuts is spelled with only four letters!

Questions, Answers & Awards

Biggest waste of time:
The "duck and cover" drills used during the 50's and 60's to help survival rates in case a nuclear attack just happened one day when you were in school!

Highest court in the land:
For those of you answering the Supreme Court of the United States, you are close. There is one court above the Supreme Court. Literally, there is a court directly above the Supreme Court. A few years ago the young staffers built a basketball court above the ceiling of the Supreme Court Chambers. Here, they were able to get some exercise when on break.

Myth:
A Union Captain in 1862 on a Civil War battlefield finds his son dead in a Confederate uniform but with musical notes in his pocket. His son had gone to a southern college to study music and got drafted. It is now the song called Taps.

Truth:
Taps was written on the battlefields in 1862 but not by a dead soldier. General Butterfield adapted an earlier bugle call at Harrison's Landing. As it was being practiced, other buglers wanted to use it and it spread throughout both armies. Later at a funeral during a possible potential battle situation, thinking that the traditional three shot volley could be misinterpreted by the enemy; *Taps* was played instead. Years after the war, that became the new tradition.

Biggest Irony:
That the girl in the song, *The Yellow Rose of Texas,* could have been a person of mixed race thus yellow as was the term of the day. A rose usually meant young woman if not actually referring to the flower. The

song was one of the favorites of the Confederate troops. The controversy is over a woman named Emily D. West. She was a free Black from Connecticut who went to work in Texas for a guy named Morgan. Some people mistakenly thought that she was Morgan's slave, and called her Emily Morgan. The story is that she and others were captured by troops of Santa Ana. Just before the Battle of San Jacinto, supposedly Emily was in Santa Ana's tent distracting him. During the battle, Santa Ana was eventually captured and Texas won its independence. While it is true that the Texans surprised Santa Ana at the Battle of San Jacinto, the reason has never been substantiated and neither has the origin of the song. It did originate at the same time but one source claimed that the original was a love song from a male slave. I doubt that story because slaves traditionally weren't taught to read let alone write music. The song was modified a bit by the Confederate troops. All of this mystery makes this great song even better.

Worst Vote in History:
Iowa's 5th District Representative on the motion for a plaque to commend the many slaves that helped build the U.S. Capital Building. In a vote of 399-1 Republican Steve King voted by himself. [1 Concurrent Resolution 135, July 7, 2009]

Worst Legislation:
The right to keep your gun if you have to declare bankruptcy. (Only if the gun is valued at less than $1500). [HR 5827/S3654 July of 2010]

Most important message:
Delivered by Pheidippides after winning the battle of Marathon and he had run 26 miles to Athens to say with his dying breath, "We won!"

Biggest question in History:
Since Pheidippides message was so important, why didn't he ride a horse?

Missed vote:

I missed the vote in 1988 on allowing the importation of Harlequin Beatles (Harmonia axyridis) commonly called lady bugs to eat aphids that were attacking the soy bean plants. Lady bugs don't seem to have any natural enemies and they are so very annoying!

Election making us look most like a third world country:

2000 Presidential election between Al Gore and George W. Bush and the hanging chad in Florida whose Governor was the winner's brother. It was close with 1876 and the back room deal for Hayes over Tilden, or the 'corrupt bargain' of 1824 with John Quincy Adams over Andrew Jackson. Both of those were more than 134 years ago and not part of the modern era.

Most far-reaching agreement with a foreign power not to receive any acknowledgement:

In 1818, Secretary of State John Quincy Adams for President Monroe got Great Britain to agree to a demilitarize zone on the American and Canadian border. The Great Lakes would be a naval war ship free zone. Remember that we had just finished fighting our second war with Great Britain and had tried to invade Canada twice.

Most Patriotic American:

From the literally millions of deserving candidates, my pick is Nathanial Hale. A school teacher turned spy. Before he was executed, he said, "I only regret that I have but one life to give for my country."

Poorest argument in legislation:

18 year olds should be able to vote since they are old enough to fight. In the old army, we wanted soldiers to follow orders and not to think. We would like voters to think. 18 year olds should be allowed to vote because they are usually graduating from high school and have just taken an American Government class and that is the better time to introduce them to voting than when they are away from home at a job or at college.

Most ingenious invention American invention:

Named the Turtle. It was invented by David Bushnell and was the world's first submarine! It was used on September 6, 1776 in a failed attack on the British Flag Ship the HMS *Eagle*. Submarine warfare doesn't become practical until WWI 138 years later.

Invention that most changed America:

The Automobile, because of the changes in transportation, need for oil and politics dealing with drilling, OPEC and the Middle East. Soon to be the combination of the computer and the internet but this hasn't had the political effect yet. The "Wikileaks" controversy will fade away and make reports more secure but boring.

Kanawha almost was the name of what state?

West Virginia

Best Toast:

A favorite toast of the early American Army was, "A hoop for the barrel!" Of course, barrel making was very common before 1800 so everyone understood that each of the staves represented a state, and together the staves made the barrel. The barrel was the United States, and the hoop that held the barrel together was the U. S. Constitution.

Where do the 'Harlem Globetrotters' come from?

No, not Harlem, it is actually Chicago. Most of the original players came from Wendell Phillips High School and played in Iowa and Illinois. To make them sound more unique and mysterious and famous, their manager Abe Saperstein came up with the new name as a marketing tool in the late 1920's and it worked.

What did emblems made out of Palmetto leaves stand for?

It showed South Carolina's support for nullification of the Tariff of Abomination 1828.

What did Admiral David Farragut really mean when he said, "Damn the torpedoes, full speed ahead!"

Torpedoes in this time period were floating mines that were tied to the bottom so that they stayed under water and couldn't be seen.

Farragut, whose first name was Jorge before he was adopted, ordered the attack to continue after a mine (torpedo) blew up and sank one of his ships. His resultant victory closed the last remaining port of the Confederacy; (Mobile Alabama) also gave us our first Hispanic hero.

Biggest mistake that turned out to be the greatest fortune:
22 year old George Washington attacks a French diplomatic party and starts the French and Indian War. To pay for the war Great Britain has to tax the colonies. The colonies resist and a revolution starts. George Washington, one of very few colonists with command experience is named leader of the revolutionary army and after the victory of the United States, he becomes the first President and is forever known as the Father of our country.

The simplest invention that caused the biggest change:
Barbed wire. From closing the open range in the West, to prison wall tops, to Pamela Anderson's tattoos.

Of our Founding Fathers, which one had the most say so?
The answer by two accounts would be Roger Sherman from Connecticut. He usually is just known for suggesting the compromise that satisfied big population states by having one house, House of Representatives, based on population. A second house, Senate, has equal representation and that satisfied the smaller states. Sherman's system has been copied by many countries and has proven to work very well. Not as well known is the fact that Roger Sherman is the only person to have signed the Constitution of the United States 1789, the Articles of Confederation and Perpetual Union 1781, the Declaration of Independence 1776, and the Continental Association of 1774.

Biggest question in American History:
Where did Uncle Sam come from? A meat packer during the War of 1812 put salted meat in barrels and marked them U.S. for United States. His name was Samuel Wilson. His usual customer was E.A. so to keep the products separate the barrels were marked. His workers weren't familiar with U.S. so one of his workers joked that the letters stood for "Uncle Sam."[70] It caught on. Soon soldiers called themselves Uncle Sam's soldiers. He stood for honesty and hard work. The United

States already had a symbol called Brother Jonathan. In 1861 Uncle Sam appeared in *Harpers* and in 1862 *Harpers* had Brother Jonathan. By 1864 Jonathan had faded away and Thomas Nast's image of Uncle Sam standing for unity and equality, survived. Uncle Sam's most famous image is his "I want you poster". It was from 1917 by James Montgomery Flagg. Flagg combined Nast's image with flag colors and a top hat and striped pants and goatee with Great Britain's Lord Kitchener's 1914 'I want you' poster. Uncle Sam did have some female competition called "Columbia". She seems to have disappeared in 1920's.

Liberty's Song

Liberty's Song by John Dickinson of Pennsylvania. Dickinson was the principle author of the Articles of Confederation and Perpetual Union. On July 4, 1768 he sent this to James Otis and to the Pennsylvania Journal on July 7. Later it was printed in the Boston Gazette. It was adapted from a British Naval Song "Heart of Oak" and an Irish emigration tune called "Here's a Health."

Come, join hand in hand, brave Americans all,
And rouse your bold hearts at fair Liberty's call;
No tyrannous acts shall suppress your just claim,
Or stain with dishonor America's name.

Chorus: In Freedom we're born and in Freedom we'll live.
Our purses are ready. Steady, friends, steady;
Not as slaves, but as Freemen our money we'll give.

Our worthy forefathers, let's give them a cheer,
To climates unknown did courageously steer;
Thro' oceans to deserts for Freedom they came,
And dying, bequeath'd us their freedom and fame.

Chorus: In Freedom we're born and in Freedom we'll live.
Our purses are ready. Steady, friends, steady;
Not as slaves, but as Freemen our money we'll give.

The tree their own hands had to Liberty rear'd,
They lived to behold growing strong and revered;
With transport they cried, Now our wishes we gain,
For our children shall gather the fruits of our pain.

Chorus: In Freedom we're born and in Freedom we'll live.
Our purses are ready. Steady, friends, steady;
Not as slaves, but as Freemen our money we'll give.

Then join hand in hand, brave Americans all,
By uniting we stand, by dividing we fall;
In so righteous a cause let us hope to succeed,
For heaven approves of each generous deed.

Chorus: In Freedom we're born and in Freedom we'll live.
Our purses are ready. Steady, friends, steady;
Not as slaves, but as Freemen our money we'll give.

Let us go forward, living these words of John Dickinson.

End notes:

1. Davidson James West. *American Nation: Beginnings to 1877.* Saddle River, NJ: Prentice Hall Inc., 1997. pg 192
2. Davidson, pg. 47
3. Davidson, pg. 87
4. Jensen, Merrill. *The Founding of a Nation: A History of the American Revolution* 1763-1776, New York: Oxford University Press, 1968. p.240-41
5. Nevins & Commager, Allan & Henry S. *A Short History of the United States.* New York: Alfred A. Knopf, 1966.
6. Schweikart L. & Allen M. *A Patriot's History of the United States,* New York: Sentinel, 2004 p70
7. Scull, Florence D. *John Dickinson Sounds the Alarm.* Philadelphia: Auerbach, 1972 p133
8. Schweikart & Allen p 109
9. Schweikart & Allen p 109
10. Stahr p107
11. *A Respectable Army, The Military Origins of the Republic,*1763-1789
    by James Kirby Martin and Mark Edward Lender, Copyright 1982
    Harlan Division, Inc. pp.186-193
12. Schachner, Nathan. *Alexander Hamilton.* New Jersey: Oak Tree Publications, 1961. Print. p273
13. Schachner, p262
14. Scull, p128
15. Davidson p257
16. Davidson p248
17. Schachner p304
18. Davidson p338
19. Remini, Robert V. *Andrew Jackson.* New York: Harper & Row, 1966.

20. Johnson, Paul. *A History of the American People.* 1st U.S. Ed. New York: Harper Collins, 1997. p.356

21. Byrd, Robert C. *Losing America.* New York: Norton & Co., 2004. p 58

22. Eicher, David J. *Dixie Betrayed.* 1st ed. New York: Little,Brown & Co., 2006.

23. Gallagher,Gary W.. *The Confederate War.* Cambridge Ma: Harvard U, 1997.

24. Davidson p. 159

25. Schweikart & Allen p514

26. Davidson p108

27. Halberstam,David. *The Fifties.* New York: Villard Books, 1993. p. 443

28. *[Copied by Justin Sanders from J.A. May & J.R. Faunt, *South Carolina Secedes* (U. of S. Car. Pr, 1960), pp. 76-81.]*

29. Allen, Michael Patrick, and Larry Schweikart. *A Patriot's History of the United States: From Columbus's Great Discovery to the War on Terror.* Reno, NV: Sentinel Hc, 2004. Print. p35

30. Schweikart L, Allen M, p305

31. Schweikart L, Allen M, p307-8

32. Oldham, William S. *Rise and Fall of the Confederacy, Memoirs' of Senator William S. Oldham CSA.* Clayton E. Jelvett. U of Missouri Press, 2006.

33. Coolidge, Olivia E. *The Statesmanship of Abraham Lincoln.* New York: Charles Scribner, 1976. p146

34. Gallagher,

35. Davidson p.492

36. Davidson p.497

37. Davidson p.492

38. Dees, Morris. & Fiffer, Steve. *Hate on Trial: The case Against America's Most Dangerous Neo-Nazi.* Villard Books, 1993. p.11

39. Davidson p.300-301

40. Matthew Josephson, *The Robber Barons: The Great American Capitalists* 1861-1901, New York: Harcourt, Brace and Company, 1934

41. Von Drehle, David. *Triangle: A Fire That Changed America.* New York: Atlantic Monthly Press, 2003. p. 119

42. Danzer p.595

43. Johnson, Paul. *A History of the American People.* New York: Harper-Collins, 1997. p.743

44. Johnson, p.742

45. Marger, Martin N. *Race and Ethnic Relations: American and Global Perspectives.* 7th ed. Belmont Ca. Thomson/Wadsworth, 2006. p.236

46. Johnson p. 780

47. Appleby p.507

48. Halberstam p.396

49. Halberstam p. 396

50. Halberstam p. 406

51. Nevins & Commager p. 599

52. Nevins & Commager p. 613

53. Schweikart & Allen p 687

54. Danzer, Klor de Alva, Krieger, Wilson, Woloch, the *Americans.* Evanston: McDougal Littell, 2009. p 1002

55. Johnson p. 918

56. Appleby, Brinkley, Broussard, McPherson, Ritchie, National Geographic, *the American Vision. Modern Times.* New York: Glencoe, 2008. p.748

57. Davis K. p 510

58. Davis p511-12

59. Schweikart & Allen p750

60. Marger, p. 365

61. Appleby p.658

62. Clarke, Richard A. *Against All Enemies.* New York: Free Press, 2004.

63. Wikipedia, the free encyclopedia, *National Debt by U.S. presidential terms.*

64. Danzer, Klor de Alva, Krieger, Wilson, Woloch, the *Americans.* Evanston: McDougal Littell, 2009. p.553

65. Langguth, A.J. *Patriots the Men Who Started the American Revolution.* New York: Simon & Schuster, 1988. p.184

66. Nevins & Commager p.74

67. p. 319 Danzer, Klor de Alva, Krieger, Wilson, Woloch, the *Americans.* Evanston: McDougal Littell, 2009.

68. Tocqueville, Alexis de. *Democracy in America.* Richard D. Heffner. New York: New American library, 1956. p112

69. Tocqueville, p55
70. Danzer, p.202

Author's Note:

As I stated before, the country is concerned with our schools and how we need to concentrate on math and sciences. Although there is always room for improvement, schools are not totally to blame as so many of our students have jobs after school or poor study habits causing poor learning. Many problems in school are not teaching as much as parenting and social attitudes. If the school climate is to draw Christmas Trees on your state or national tests such as the Iowa Test of Educational Development, then one is not trying to learn very much.

This is a picture of me teaching in 1977, and it is the way I think of myself in my mind. The real me is on the back cover. Originally I planned to use this picture there but there is a problem... see it?

I went to a company to have this picture made from a slide. It was finished at closing time so I didn't get a chance to look at it. Obviously to you the reader, Europe is backwards. To us it just jumps out but to the person on the job, it was just a picture of a guy.

To me, it is proof of our need to put more emphasis on Social Studies!

Thanks for reading this book.